The History of Scotland

CRAFTED BY SKRIUWER

Copyright © 2024 by Skriuwer.

All rights reserved. No part of this book may be used or reproduced in any form whatsoever without written permission except in the case of brief quotations in critical articles or reviews.

For more information, contact : **kontakt@skriuwer.com** (www.skriuwer.com)

TABLE OF CONTENTS

CHAPTER 1: PREHISTORIC SCOTLAND

Earliest inhabitants and environment
Mesolithic to Neolithic transitions
Formation of early communities and monument building
Bronze Age society and technology

CHAPTER 2: THE IRON AGE AND THE RISE OF TRIBAL SOCIETIES

Expansion of ironworking and hillforts
Formation of tribal identities and defense
Daily life, crafts, and trade networks
Transition leading to Roman encounters

CHAPTER 3: ROMAN INFLUENCE IN CALEDONIA

Agricola's campaigns and Mons Graupius
Construction of forts, roads, and defensive walls
Impact on local tribes and Roman retreat
Legacy of Roman roads and cultural exchange

CHAPTER 4: THE AGE OF THE PICTS

Origins and significance of Pictish kingdoms
Symbol stones, art, and religious transitions
Political dynamics with neighboring groups
Rise of the Gaels and later interactions

CHAPTER 5: THE ARRIVAL OF THE GAELS AND THE KINGDOM OF DALRIADA

Origins from Ireland and early settlements
Formation of Dalriada and Gaelic society
Religious influence of St. Columba and Iona
Interactions with Picts and local power shifts

CHAPTER 6: THE FORMATION OF THE EARLY SCOTTISH KINGDOM

Unification of Picts and Gaels
Role of key monarchs and alliances
Early governance structures and legal customs
Foundations for the later Kingdom of Alba

CHAPTER 7: THE VIKING INVASIONS AND INFLUENCE

Norse raids on coastal regions
Establishment of Norse settlements and Orkney earldoms
Effects on trade, language, and local power
Integration and resistance among Gaelic communities

CHAPTER 8: THE EMERGENCE OF THE KINGDOM OF ALBA

Consolidation of Pictish and Gaelic realms
MacAlpin lineage and political unification
Impact of external threats and internal reforms
Rise of a distinct Scottish monarchy

CHAPTER 9: THE REIGN OF MACBETH AND THE IMPACT OF THE NORMANS

Real Macbeth versus legend
Struggles for the throne and shifting alliances
Early Norman influences on feudal structures
Foundations for later medieval developments

CHAPTER 10: SCOTLAND'S WARS OF INDEPENDENCE

Overthrow of John Balliol and rise of William Wallace
Key battles like Stirling Bridge and Falkirk
Robert the Bruce's triumph at Bannockburn
Legacy of nationalism and treaty outcomes

CHAPTER 11: ROBERT THE BRUCE AND THE STRUGGLE FOR POWER

Bruce's lineage and path to the throne
Military campaigns against internal and external rivals
Diplomatic achievements and alliances
Rebuilding governance after Bannockburn

CHAPTER 12: THE STEWART DYNASTY TAKES SHAPE

Succession after David II and rise of Robert II
Power of the duke of Albany and regencies
Development of feudal governance and court culture
Growing tension between crown and nobility

CHAPTER 13: THE REFORMATION AND RELIGIOUS STRIFE

Influence of Protestant doctrines from Europe
Opposition to Catholic regents and Queen Mary
Knox, the Lords of the Congregation, and 1560 Parliament
Establishment of a Presbyterian Kirk

CHAPTER 14: THE UNION OF THE CROWNS

James VI's accession to the English throne
Absentee monarch and impact on Scottish governance
Religious implications and moderate episcopacy
Seeds of tension for future conflicts

CHAPTER 15: THE COVENANTERS AND CIVIL WAR

Opposition to Charles I's religious impositions
National Covenant and Bishops' Wars
Role in the wider Wars of the Three Kingdoms
Covenanter regime and subsequent collapse

CHAPTER 16: THE GLORIOUS REVOLUTION AND THE JACOBITES

Overthrow of James VII in Scotland
Installation of William and Mary, Presbyterian settlement
Early Jacobite risings like Killiecrankie and Glencoe
Tensions leading to the Act of Union debates

CHAPTER 17: THE ACTS OF UNION 1707 AND CHANGING IDENTITIES

Negotiations and economic pressures post-Darien
Scottish Parliament's abolition and new British framework
Immediate backlash and shifting national identity
Seeds for industrial expansion and enlightenment

CHAPTER 18: THE SCOTTISH ENLIGHTENMENT

Rise of Hume, Smith, Reid, and other thinkers
Intellectual societies in Edinburgh and Glasgow
Impact on philosophy, economics, and moral theory
Enduring legacy of rational inquiry and global influence

CHAPTER 19: THE IMPACT OF THE INDUSTRIAL REVOLUTION

Textile mills, coal, iron, and steel expansion
Urban growth in Glasgow and central belt
Working-class emergence, social conditions, and labor unrest
Highland–Lowland disparities and partial modernization

CHAPTER 20: REFORM, EMIGRATION, AND A CHANGING SCOTLAND

19th-century parliamentary reforms and Chartism
Clearances, Highland diaspora, and global emigration
Religious schisms like the 1843 Disruption
Evolving politics, civic institutions, and national consciousness

CHAPTER 1

PREHISTORIC SCOTLAND: THE FIRST PEOPLE

1. Introduction to Prehistoric Scotland

Prehistoric Scotland is a land of mystery and wonder. Long before written records, people roamed these rugged landscapes, hunting, gathering, and later farming. They learned to adapt to a changing climate, shifting coastlines, and thick forests. They left behind tools, weapons, and monuments made of stone. By studying these artifacts, archaeologists have been able to piece together an image of Scotland's earliest societies. Although many details remain a mystery, the evidence shows a long process of adaptation and innovation that set the stage for everything that followed.

The period we call "prehistory" refers to all the millennia before written records were kept. In Scotland, this stretches back many thousands of years. When the last Ice Age retreated, it gradually exposed more usable land. As the glaciers melted, the sea levels rose, shaping Scotland's coastline and creating places like the western isles and the northern isles. The interplay between sea and land influenced how people traveled, found food, and built settlements. Prehistoric communities in Scotland had to deal with these shifts while learning to make the most of local resources.

Early humans were drawn to Scotland's coasts and rivers for fishing, hunting, and foraging. They made temporary camps and moved with the seasons, following animal herds and searching for shellfish. Over time, some groups started to settle in more permanent locations, especially once they began domesticating animals and cultivating grains. By the time we get to the Neolithic period, we start seeing the construction of stone monuments and more stable living patterns. These changes illustrate a major transition from nomadic lifestyles to more rooted communities that would shape prehistoric Scotland into a place of vibrant cultural expression.

2. The Mesolithic Era: First Inhabitants and Their Environment

After the last Ice Age, around 10,000 BCE, small bands of hunter-gatherers began to explore the territory that would become Scotland. These people are part of what we call the Mesolithic, or Middle Stone Age. At first, the region was covered by thick forests of pine, oak, and birch. The soil was often damp, and the climate was cooler than it is today, though it gradually warmed. Rivers teemed with fish, while deer and boar wandered the forests. For these Mesolithic groups, survival meant following game animals, collecting wild fruits, and adapting to the land's seasonal changes.

They made stone tools by chipping and shaping flint or other local rocks. These tools included scrapers for working animal hides, blades for cutting, and microliths that could be set into wooden shafts to form arrows and spears. The Mesolithic people had limited technology by later standards, but they were skilled at using every resource available. They fashioned bone harpoons for fishing and used driftwood or local timber to craft canoes for traveling along coasts and rivers. Mesolithic stone tools are found across Scotland in places like the island of Rum and sites along the eastern coast, suggesting a wide spread of small communities.

Archaeological evidence also shows that these early groups did not simply wander aimlessly. They returned to favored spots year after year, following patterns of migration linked to animals, fish runs, and plant harvests. Small shelters, often ephemeral, could be built quickly, but they left traces such as post holes and charcoal deposits. One key site is at Cramond, near Edinburgh, where remnants of a Mesolithic camp reveal the presence of hunter-gatherers as early as 8,500 BCE. This camp, and others like it, shows how these early people used natural resources. They prepared hides, cooked fish, and fashioned tools. Their economy was based on a close relationship with nature, which continued for centuries.

---

3. Transition from Mesolithic to Neolithic

Over time, new ideas and practices spread into Scotland. We often call this shift the "Neolithic Revolution," though it was not an overnight change. It began roughly around 4,000 BCE, when communities across the British Isles started adopting farming, animal husbandry, and pottery. These changes likely came through contact with farming peoples moving north and west, but how exactly it happened remains under debate among archaeologists. Some think settlers from continental Europe arrived with seeds and livestock, while others argue that local hunter-gatherers slowly learned these new techniques through trade and social networks.

Either way, the Neolithic brought a new way of life. People started to settle more permanently in one place, which led to the building of stronger, longer-lasting homes. They grew crops like barley and wheat, and they kept animals such as sheep and cattle. This shift toward agriculture meant that communities could produce surplus food, store it, and develop more complex social structures. They also began making pottery for cooking and storage. Fragments of these early clay vessels, decorated with simple patterns, have been found in many prehistoric sites across Scotland. The Neolithic period thus marked a decisive break from the purely hunter-gatherer lifestyle that had defined Scottish prehistory for thousands of years.

Another hallmark of this era was the building of large stone monuments, which appeared across Scotland. These include chambered cairns, standing stones, and stone circles. They suggest new forms of ritual, belief, or social organization that had not existed in the Mesolithic. While the exact purposes of these monuments remain partly mysterious, they indicate a society that was concerned with marking the land, remembering ancestors, and possibly performing communal ceremonies. This transformation in architecture and shared practices is often seen as the dawn of a more organized, stable society.

---

4. Neolithic Settlements: Skara Brae and Other Sites

One of the best examples of a well-preserved Neolithic settlement in Scotland is Skara Brae, located on the largest island of Orkney, called Mainland. This site, discovered in the mid-19th century after a storm exposed the remains, dates back to around 3,200 BCE. Skara Brae consists of several interconnected stone houses, each with a central hearth, stone furniture such as beds and shelving, and small compartments for storage. Passageways link the homes, and each dwelling is partly sunken into the ground for insulation against Orkney's cold winds.

Skara Brae provides a remarkable look at Neolithic life. While wood was scarce in Orkney, local sandstone was plentiful and easy to shape. The inhabitants built their homes using this stone, creating walls that remain today. The settlement's layout suggests a community-based lifestyle, where neighbors lived close together, likely sharing tasks and resources. Artifacts found at the site include decorated pottery, stone tools, and items made from bone or antler. Personal ornaments, such as beads, give us a glimpse into how these early farmers and fishers expressed identity.

Other important Neolithic sites in Orkney include the Knap of Howar on the island of Papa Westray, which predates Skara Brae by a few hundred years. The Ness of Brodgar is another remarkable complex, featuring monumental stone walls and buildings that may have served as religious or ceremonial centers. These sites, along with stone circles like the Ring of Brodgar and the Stones of Stenness, show that Orkney was a vibrant hub of Neolithic culture. Although Orkney is often in the spotlight because of its stunning preservation, similar Neolithic communities existed across mainland Scotland, the Hebrides, and the northern isles.

---

5. Ceremonial Monuments and Ritual Landscapes

A key part of Neolithic Scotland was the construction of ceremonial sites that still captivate visitors today. Standing stones, stone circles, and burial cairns appear in many regions, from the islands to the mainland. Some of the famous stone circles include Callanish on the Isle of Lewis, which stands in an alignment that some researchers believe was connected to lunar or solar events. These sites often have special alignments that may have related to tracking seasons, honoring ancestors, or performing rituals.

Chambered cairns, like the Maeshowe in Orkney, are another feature of this landscape. Built as burial tombs, they often contain carefully aligned passages that allow sunlight to enter at specific times of the year, such as the winter solstice. This alignment suggests sophisticated knowledge of the sun's movement and an interest in marking key turning points of the seasonal cycle. Inside these tombs, archaeologists have found the remains of individuals who were placed there over time, sometimes with grave goods or pottery. These burials likely served as a link between the living and their ancestors, reinforcing communal bonds and traditions.

The building of these monuments required significant effort and organization. Stones had to be quarried, transported, and arranged with precision. Communities needed to cooperate, which implies strong social structures and shared beliefs. While we do not know all the details, these monuments point to a society that took ritual and memory seriously. They may have served as gathering places, where important decisions, festivals, or ceremonies occurred. Over the centuries, some monuments were adapted or reused, showing that later generations also respected and maintained their ancestors' sacred sites.

---

6. The Role of Art, Pottery, and Early Trade

Art in Neolithic Scotland often appeared in simple motifs carved on stone or pottery. Geometric patterns like spirals, lozenges, or circles appear on stone walls, megaliths, and pots. Though basic, these patterns may have held symbolic meaning. For example, spirals and circles could represent cycles of life, the sun, or the changing seasons. Such designs might have been part of rituals or linked to broader beliefs about the natural world.

Pottery was another major technological step forward. Early pots from the Neolithic were handmade, baked in open fires or simple kilns, and decorated with impressions or incisions. These vessels could be used to store grain, cook food, or transport water. Over time, pottery designs became more varied, with more detailed motifs. This variety in style might indicate regional identities or exchanges of ideas between different groups across Scotland and beyond. Fragments of pottery found at multiple sites help archaeologists trace connections between distant communities, showing that people were not isolated but shared a network of knowledge, trade, and culture.

Trade during the Neolithic was not about large-scale commerce but rather small-scale exchanges of valuable materials or finished products. Flint, for instance, was important for making tools and was not available everywhere. Communities in areas with good flint supplies could trade it to neighbors in return for other goods like animal hides or finished pots. The movement of particular stone types from one region to another also suggests that items such as polished stone axes were part of a widespread network of exchange. Some of the prized stones used for axe-heads came from special quarries, indicating that these items may have had symbolic or prestige value.

---

7. Arrival of Metal: The Bronze Age Begins

Around 2,000 BCE, metalworking reached Scotland, ushering in what we call the Bronze Age. This technology spread from continental Europe to the British Isles. The ability to cast bronze weapons, tools, and ornaments brought a major shift in how people worked, fought, and displayed status. Bronze tools could cut, carve, and dig more effectively than stone, making tasks like clearing forests or woodworking easier. At the same time, bronze weapons like swords, spears, and daggers brought changes to warfare, hunting, and leadership.

Bronze is an alloy of copper and tin. Neither metal is widely found in Scotland, so raw materials or finished objects had to be traded or carried in from elsewhere. This reliance on imported metal may have increased the importance of long-distance connections and social ties. Communities that controlled or facilitated the flow of copper or tin might have gained wealth or influence. Archaeologists have found hoards of bronze objects buried in the ground, sometimes interpreted as ritual offerings. These caches might also have been a way to store valuables for later use, or to show devotion to certain deities or ancestral spirits.

Despite the new metal technology, stone tools continued to be used. The transition did not happen overnight. People combined stone, bone, and bronze technologies according to their needs, resources, and traditions. Over the course of the Bronze Age, however, metal items became more common, and their designs grew more sophisticated. Metal ornaments, such as arm rings, brooches, and dress pins, appear in archaeological records, reflecting the rise of more visible social distinctions. These ornaments might have been a way for certain individuals or families to show wealth or rank, hinting at deeper class divisions or power structures forming within communities.

---

8. Changing Social Patterns in the Bronze Age

The Bronze Age saw changes not only in tools and weapons but also in settlement patterns and social organization. As agriculture improved, communities needed more land to raise animals and grow crops. This led to further clearing of forests, especially in more fertile regions. Farming techniques advanced, and some groups built roundhouses—circular dwellings of wood or stone, often with conical roofs of thatch. These houses could be clustered together, forming small villages in some areas. In other places, people lived in single farmsteads or scattered settlements, depending on local conditions.

Burial practices changed in the Bronze Age as well. Instead of large communal tombs like the chambered cairns of the Neolithic, people began to bury their dead in individual or small-group graves. These often took the form of cists—stone-lined burial boxes—or barrows, which were earthen mounds. Alongside the deceased, grave goods like pottery, weapons, or ornaments might be placed. These items could reflect the person's role in life or their status. The shift away from communal tombs might indicate an increased focus on the individual or on family lineage, revealing new layers of social complexity.

In some parts of Scotland, archaeologists have found evidence of small hillforts or fortified enclosures that date to the Late Bronze Age. These sites might have served as defense against raids, or they could have been symbols of status and control by a local leader. While we do not see the large-scale, highly stratified societies found in later periods, there is a sense that power was becoming more centralized. Control over metal resources, arable land, or strategic trade routes could elevate certain families or clans. These social changes paved the way for greater regional identity and laid foundations for Iron Age tribal structures.

---

9. Daily Life, Diet, and Cultural Practices

For the average person in Bronze Age Scotland, life involved a balance of farming, herding, and local crafting. People raised cattle, sheep, goats, and, in some areas, pigs. They planted barley, wheat, and possibly oats, though yields were dependent on climate and soil quality. Fishing and gathering shellfish remained important, especially in coastal areas. Hunting deer and wild boar was still practiced, though domesticated sources of food had become more reliable. A varied diet of grains, meat, fish, and gathered plants helped communities survive the seasonal changes and occasional poor harvests.

Craftspeople in the Bronze Age were skilled at pottery-making, weaving, and metalworking. Weavers used wool from sheep to create textiles, which might be dyed using local plants to produce simple colors. Pottery styles became more elaborate, with decorated beakers or urns that could be placed in graves or used for storage. Metalworkers, often seen as specialists, could cast bronze tools, blades, and ornaments. These skills likely gave them a higher status in some communities. At the same time, everyday labor was shared among men and women, with tasks divided according to tradition, season, and need.

Ritual and religion continued to evolve. Certain natural sites like springs, bogs, or lakes might have been revered as sacred places where offerings were made. Metal objects found in bog deposits could be seen as ritual gifts to gods or spirits that were associated with water and fertility. Some Bronze Age sites show evidence of wooden platforms or causeways built out into wetlands, possibly for ceremonial purposes. The presence of burnt offerings, special pottery, and arranged items indicate that spiritual life was deeply woven into the routine of these communities. As with many parts of prehistoric religion, the specifics remain unclear, but the archaeological evidence suggests that people were keen to maintain a connection with the unseen forces they believed influenced harvests, health, and well-being.

---

10. Environmental Challenges and Adaptation
Even though the climate in the Bronze Age was generally milder than in the Mesolithic, communities still had to adapt to environmental challenges. Periods of colder or wetter weather could harm crops, while storms might damage settlements along coasts. In some cases, people abandoned certain areas when the soil became exhausted or when resources grew scarce. Archaeological layers sometimes show phases of decline followed by new waves of settlement, hinting at a cycle of adaptation. Wetlands and boggy ground preserved many organic materials, giving us more information about what people grew and ate, as well as how they built and repaired tools and shelters.

Some of the changes in settlement patterns can be linked to shifting coastlines. Rising sea levels in some areas might have forced communities to relocate or adjust their farming methods. In other parts of Scotland, people used raised beaches or sheltered inlets for fishing and small boats. Access to marine resources remained vital, with shell middens (large piles of discarded shells) showing how important seafood was for coastal groups. Inland, forests were cut down to create farmland, which had a lasting impact on wildlife and the ecosystem. Over time, these changes in land use might have contributed to erosion or soil depletion, pushing people to find new locations or new ways of living.

Through these challenges, Bronze Age communities displayed resourcefulness. They refined farming practices, rotated crops, and sometimes built small drainage systems. They developed new building techniques for houses and storage areas, ensuring they could better endure wet conditions. While life was still tough by modern standards, the archaeological record shows a gradual increase in the sophistication of tools, housing, and social structures. This resilience laid a strong foundation for the next major shift: the Iron Age, which would bring further technological change and new forms of social organization.

---

11. End of the Bronze Age and the Dawn of the Iron Age
By around 800 BCE, the use of iron tools had started to appear in parts of Britain. In Scotland, this transition took time, varying by region. Some groups continued to rely on bronze for weapons and ornaments, while others adopted iron more quickly. Iron ore could often be found closer to where people lived, reducing the reliance on long-distance trade for tin or copper. Iron tools were stronger and more durable. They could be sharpened repeatedly, unlike bronze, which was softer and wore down faster. This advantage in durability and cutting ability meant that communities with iron technology could clear more land, build more effectively, and potentially outperform neighbors in warfare or hunting.

The end of the Bronze Age was not a simple event but a gradual transformation that led into what we call the Iron Age. The changes in materials, economy, and social structures created new opportunities and challenges. In some areas, hillforts expanded or were refurbished with more robust defenses. People continued to craft decorative objects from bronze, gold, or other metals, but iron came to dominate practical tools. Over time, the tribes that would define Iron Age Scotland began to form more distinct identities, influenced by both internal developments and contacts with lands to the south and across the sea.

By looking at this long arc from the Mesolithic through the Bronze Age, we can see how the foundation of Scotland's prehistory was built. The shift from nomadic hunting to settled farming, the rise of monumental architecture, the spread of metalworking, and the growth of social complexity all influenced how people would live in the coming centuries. Scotland was not an isolated place, even in these early times. Ideas, goods, and people moved across land and water, shaping a vibrant tapestry of cultures. These early foundations set the stage for the next phase of Scotland's story: the Iron Age and the rise of tribal societies, which we will explore in the following chapter.

CHAPTER 2

THE IRON AGE AND THE RISE OF TRIBAL SOCIETIES

1. Introduction to the Iron Age

The Iron Age in Scotland spans roughly from 800 BCE to the arrival of the Romans in the 1st century CE, though exact dates vary across regions. During this period, iron replaced bronze as the primary metal for tools and weapons. This transition had far-reaching effects on agriculture, settlement patterns, social organization, and warfare. Iron tools were cheaper to produce once people learned to smelt and forge the metal. While bronze still had a place for decorative items and status symbols, iron quickly became essential for everyday tasks like plowing, building, and fighting.

This era also saw the emergence of more defined tribal groups. People started to gather in larger communities, often protected by hillforts or defended enclosures. These fortified sites became power centers where leaders could display their influence. We can see evidence of social stratification through the range of artifacts and the scale of hillfort construction. Some hillforts were small, with simple ramparts and ditches, while others had multiple lines of defenses. We also see changes in house styles, with roundhouses becoming common across much of Scotland. These structures were built to suit a range of climates and were often grouped within fortified walls, suggesting the importance of security and communal living.

---

2. Ironworking and Its Impacts

The key development driving the Iron Age was the mastery of iron smelting and forging. Iron ore could be found in various parts of Scotland, though the quality and quantity differed by region. Iron production required higher temperatures than bronze working, so specialized furnaces called bloomeries were used. Workers packed iron ore and charcoal into these furnaces, then pumped in air with bellows. The result was a spongy mass of iron called a "bloom," which was then hammered to remove impurities and shaped into tools or weapons.

The availability of iron changed the balance of power. Bronze had relied on copper and tin, often imported from afar. Iron could be sourced more locally, at least to some extent, which meant communities might gain independence from long-distance trade routes. That said, iron production was still not easy. It required skill, organization, and enough labor to gather ore and maintain the charcoal supply. Some regions emerged as centers of ironworking, attracting skilled smiths and possibly controlling local trade. Iron tools increased agricultural productivity, allowing farmers to till heavier soils and clear forests more efficiently. This, in turn, could support larger populations and more specialized crafts.

Iron weapons also changed warfare. Swords and spears made from iron were stronger than their bronze counterparts and could be produced in greater numbers. Warriors who had access to good quality iron might dominate rivals still relying on older technology. This shift could lead to more territorial expansion, alliances, or conflicts among emerging tribes. Over time, the presence of iron brought new confidence in constructing fortifications, as the tools to carve ditches and shape wooden palisades became more effective. In this way, iron influenced not just the economy but the social and political fabric of Iron Age Scotland.

---

3. Hillforts and Brochs: Symbols of Power and Defense
As we move deeper into the Iron Age, we see an increase in the construction of defended sites such as hillforts and brochs. Hillforts are typically situated on elevated ground, taking advantage of natural slopes for defense. Ramparts, ditches, and wooden or stone walls were built to keep out attackers. Some hillforts in Scotland, like Eildon Hill North in the Borders or Tap O' Noth in Aberdeenshire, could encompass large areas, suggesting a concentration of population or a place of refuge. The size and complexity of these structures often reflect the power of local leaders who could organize labor and resources on a grand scale.

Brochs, on the other hand, are unique to Scotland. They are tall, circular stone towers found mostly in the northern and western parts of the country. They date primarily to the later Iron Age (roughly from 200 BCE to 200 CE). Brochs often stand near the coast or in prominent positions, and their thick double-walled design provided both shelter and defense. Inside, they might have wooden floors or platforms, creating multiple levels of living space. The exact purpose of brochs is still debated. Some believe they were high-status dwellings for local chiefs or important families. Others argue they were communal refuges, storing supplies and protecting people during raids. Whatever their function, these impressive stone towers are a hallmark of Iron Age Scotland, showcasing advanced building techniques and a concern for security.

In addition to hillforts and brochs, there were also smaller defended homesteads and duns—stone-walled structures often found in the Highlands and Islands. These varied sites indicate that Iron Age societies were sometimes wary of conflict, or at least wanted to display strength. At the same time, they might serve as a statement of wealth or status, signaling that the community's leader had the resources and authority to command large-scale building efforts. Trade and travel along the coasts and rivers likely connected these sites, fostering a sense of shared culture despite regional differences in architecture and customs.

---

4. Daily Life in Iron Age Villages
While hillforts and brochs represent dramatic examples of Iron Age architecture, many people lived in simpler farmsteads scattered across the countryside. Roundhouses were common, built using timber or stone walls with conical thatched roofs. These dwellings were designed to withstand Scotland's damp and windy climate. Inside, a central hearth provided heat and a place to cook. Depending on the size of the household, living space might be divided into areas for sleeping, storage, and food preparation. Cattle, sheep, and sometimes pigs were kept, and fields of barley and oats were planted around the settlement. In coastal areas, fishing and gathering shellfish remained vital.

The Iron Age diet likely included breads or porridges made from grain, supplemented by meat, dairy products, and wild resources like berries or wild game. Seasonal rhythms dictated much of life. Spring meant planting crops and birthing livestock. Summer was a time of growth and grazing. Autumn brought the harvest and preparation for winter, with people storing grains, drying fish, and salting or smoking meat. Winter was harsh, especially in the north. Communities had to survive on preserved foods and rely on stored fodder for their animals. Festive gatherings and communal feasting might help maintain social bonds during the dark, cold months. These events also reinforced loyalties to local leaders, who might distribute food and drink in exchange for support.

Clothing was woven from wool, sometimes dyed in simple colors using natural pigments. Leather was used for shoes, belts, and other practical items. Jewelry such as brooches, armlets, or torcs (neck rings) was made from bronze or iron, and in some cases from precious metals like gold. Such items could signify status or affiliation with a particular group. Everyday tools included iron sickles for harvesting, iron axes for chopping wood, and stone or wooden implements for grinding grain. Life in these villages was not luxurious, but the introduction of iron helped communities handle the demands of farming, building, and defending themselves in a challenging environment.

---

5. Iron Age Society: Tribes, Hierarchies, and Customs

The Iron Age saw a rise in more defined tribal identities. Although written records about early Scottish tribes are scarce, later Roman sources mention names like the Caledonii, Maeatae, and others who lived north of the Roman frontier. Each tribe would have been made up of smaller clans or groups, bound by kinship and allegiance to a chieftain or king. Hillforts, brochs, and other defended sites might serve as tribal centers, where assemblies were held or where goods were traded.

Social hierarchy appears to have been more pronounced during the Iron Age. Elites or chieftains controlled more resources, including the best land and valuable items like imported wine or decorated metalwork. They could host large feasts, rewarding warriors or allies, and collecting tribute from the surrounding countryside. Warriors, in turn, sought to gain honor through bravery in battle or by raiding rival tribes. The possession of iron weaponry and armor could elevate a warrior's status. Meanwhile, craftspeople like blacksmiths, potters, and weavers held vital roles, even if they did not typically wield political power. Farmers and herders made up the bulk of the population, ensuring a stable food supply.

Customs and laws were likely handed down orally. Tribal elders or druids (in some Celtic-speaking areas) might have been guardians of these traditions. Although direct evidence of druids in Scotland is limited, parallels with other Celtic societies suggest that religious specialists or wise individuals existed. Rituals might involve offerings of food, weapons, or valuable objects in natural places like pools, rivers, or bogs. Certain sites might have been considered sacred groves or hills, where seasonal festivals or tribal councils took place. These cultural practices knitted Iron Age communities together, creating a sense of shared identity that set them apart from neighboring peoples.

---

6. Art and Craftsmanship in the Iron Age
Iron Age art in Scotland reflected broader Celtic influences. Complex swirling patterns, stylized animals, and intricate knotwork would later become even more elaborate in the Pictish and early medieval periods. In the Iron Age, we see early forms of these motifs on metal objects, such as decorated scabbards, shields, or brooches. Pottery continued to be functional, though less ornate than in some earlier periods. The introduction of the potter's wheel was slow, and hand-built pottery remained common in many regions.

Metalworkers produced a range of items, including tools, weapons, and jewelry. Bronze casting did not disappear; instead, iron and bronze were used side by side. Elite items could showcase fine craftsmanship. For instance, a bronze shield might be inlaid with enamel or engraved with geometric designs. Warrior equipment, such as sword hilts, could feature detailed metalwork, highlighting the owner's rank. Some decorative objects, like the famous "Gundestrup Cauldron" found in Denmark, show how far Celtic art could travel or be influenced by distant cultures, though that specific artifact is not from Scotland. Still, the broad Celtic art style was part of an expansive network of trade and cultural exchange that included much of Europe.

Local materials remained important. Iron Age artisans used jet (a type of fossilized wood) from parts of Britain for beads or small ornaments. They also carved bone or antler for tools and decorative elements. Glass bead-making might have been practiced, producing colorful beads for necklaces or bracelets. These crafts not only enhanced daily life but also served as symbols of status or group identity. They were often traded as gifts or tribute, forging alliances among tribes and connecting Scotland with other Celtic cultures across the British Isles and continental Europe.

---

7. Trade and External Contacts

Though Scotland was far from the Mediterranean world, there is evidence of external contacts and trade during the Iron Age. Items like Roman pottery, glass, or even luxury foods like wine could find their way to tribal elites, especially in the southern parts of Scotland, by the late Iron Age. Some coastal settlements or islands might have maintained trading links with Irish or Atlantic seafaring communities. Traveling traders could exchange exotic goods for locally produced textiles, skins, metalwork, or possibly slaves.

These contacts were not always peaceful. Raiding and warfare could also be part of the Iron Age experience, as tribes competed for resources, land, or prestige. Still, the movement of goods and ideas suggests that Iron Age Scotland was part of a wider cultural network. The spread of Celtic languages, art styles, and religious practices across western Europe may have reached Scotland through these connections. While we cannot be sure how extensive this communication was, archaeological finds such as Mediterranean pottery in certain hillforts or brochs point to the influence of distant lands on local elites.

---

8. Religious Beliefs and Ritual Practices

Direct knowledge of Iron Age religious beliefs in Scotland is limited, but material evidence suggests a reverence for natural elements and possibly for ancestors or deities tied to aspects of the environment. Offerings in bogs or rivers could represent attempts to appease gods, gain blessings, or honor the memory of important individuals. Weapons deliberately broken or bent before being deposited might indicate a ritual "killing" of the object, preventing its reuse and devoting it to the gods. Some burial practices also show care in how bodies were laid to rest, with occasional grave goods or tokens symbolizing status or spiritual significance.

Sacred groves, springs, or hilltops might have served as gathering places for community rites. Druids, if they existed similarly to those in Gaul or

Ireland, might have guided religious ceremonies and oral traditions. They possibly performed sacrifices—animal or, in rare cases, human—though evidence of human sacrifice is hard to confirm in the Scottish context. Artistic depictions of gods or mythic scenes are rare in the Iron Age of Scotland, but we see a few figurines or carvings that might suggest veneration of warrior gods, mother goddesses, or symbols representing fertility and protection. Without written records, much remains guesswork, but it's clear that religion played a vital role in reinforcing community bonds and explaining the forces of nature.

---

9. Social Conflict and Warfare

Iron Age warfare in Scotland likely varied from small-scale raiding to occasional larger conflicts between tribes. The presence of hillforts and brochs indicates a concern for defense. These strongholds provided refuge during attacks, and their construction might have been a communal effort that united the tribe under powerful leaders. Raiders might seize cattle, slaves, or valuable goods. Skirmishes could arise over disputed grazing lands or control of trade routes. Weapons such as iron swords, spears, and sometimes slings were used. Leather shields or wooden shields with metal fittings provided some protection, although full armor was rare.

Warriors sought to prove their bravery, earning status and possibly gaining loot to distribute among followers. Feasting after successful raids or battles could strengthen loyalty to a chieftain. Storytelling around the hearth fire might celebrate heroes of past engagements, building a sense of collective identity. The discovery of so-called "warrior burials" in some areas, containing weapons and ornaments, points to the importance of martial prowess. However, we must not assume that Iron Age Scotland was in a constant state of conflict. Trading alliances, intermarriage between tribes, and shared religious customs could foster periods of peace and cooperation. The threat of violence was never far away, but communities balanced warfare with farming, trade, and daily survival.

---

10. Regional Differences Within Iron Age Scotland

Scotland's varied geography—ranging from fertile Lowlands to rugged Highlands, from coastline to deep inland valleys—shaped local cultures during the Iron Age. In the south and east, closer ties with other parts of Britain might have existed, whether friendly or hostile. Tribes there might have had earlier access to Roman goods or influences. In the north and western isles, the prominence of brochs suggests a different style of fortification, possibly adapted to local resources and the need to defend against seaborne threats. The Gaelic-speaking communities of later periods may have had roots in these Iron Age groups that navigated Atlantic networks and lived in stone structures adapted to harsh coastal weather.

The Highlands, with their mountainous terrain, might have supported smaller, scattered communities focused on herding and localized agriculture. Weather extremes and limited arable land could have restricted the size and power of these groups, though they maintained a unique cultural identity. Crannogs—artificial islands built in lochs—are another form of dwelling found in some areas. They date to various times, including the Iron Age, and could serve as secure homesteads. Each region thus put its own stamp on Iron Age life, creating a patchwork of societies bound together by certain shared technologies (ironworking, roundhouse building) but differentiated by local resources and traditions.

---

11. The Late Iron Age and the Approach of Rome

By the late Iron Age, Scotland's tribal societies had established networks of alliances and rivalries. Leaders of larger tribes might exert influence over smaller neighboring groups. Some engaged in trade with tribes farther south, potentially exchanging cattle, hides, or metalwork for Roman imports. Yet for many communities, life continued much as before: farming, fishing, herding, and defending territory. Then came a monumental shift—Rome began to expand its Empire into Britain in the 1st century CE. Julius Caesar's expeditions in the south of Britain in 55 and 54 BCE did not reach Scotland, but they opened the door to future campaigns.

During the reign of Emperor Claudius, the Roman conquest of southern Britain advanced northward, reaching the territory of various British tribes. By the 70s CE, Rome's legions were pressing into northern England and looking further into the lands of the Caledonii and other Scottish tribes. This would mark the first major incursion of Rome into Scotland, leading to battles like Mons Graupius around 83 CE, described by the Roman historian

Tacitus. Though not everyone in Scotland would have been directly affected at first, the mere presence of Rome so close to tribal lands foretold the next big transformation in Scottish history.

---

12. Transition to the Next Era
The Iron Age in Scotland set the stage for the dramatic encounters that would define the next chapters of the nation's story. Tribal societies had their own ways of life, anchored by roundhouses, hillforts, brochs, and a reliance on iron tools. Agriculture and herding kept communities fed, while local elites sought prestige through warfare, feasting, and displays of wealth. Artisans honed their skills, and some groups engaged in trade networks extending beyond the seas. Religion and ritual practices tied communities together, shaping their worldviews and sustaining social bonds.

As the Romans prepared to push into Caledonia, Scotland's tribes faced new threats and opportunities. Some leaders might have seen an alliance with Rome as a chance to gain power over rivals. Others resisted fiercely to protect their land and freedom. Regardless of which path they chose, the arrival of Rome would usher in an era of upheaval. Hillforts and brochs would face siege or adaptation, trade routes might expand or shift, and local power structures could collapse or re-emerge in new forms. This clash of cultures between Rome and Iron Age Scotland will be the focus of our next chapters, providing a glimpse into the resilience and adaptability that have come to define Scottish history.

CHAPTER 3

ROMAN INFLUENCE IN CALEDONIA

1. Introduction

By the late Iron Age, Scotland—known to the Romans as "Caledonia"—was home to various tribes. They were skilled farmers, herders, and warriors who lived in fortified hillforts, brochs, and smaller settlements. Trade and cultural ties connected them to neighboring regions, yet life was still shaped by the local landscape and seasonal changes. Around the 1st century CE, a major force entered the scene: the Roman Empire, which was expanding northward after gaining control of much of southern Britain.

Roman interest in Caledonia brought new military campaigns, fortifications, and interactions with local tribes. Although the Romans never fully conquered all of Scotland, their presence left a mark on the region's political structures and economy. In this chapter, we will explore the key campaigns, the building of forts and walls, and how Roman involvement influenced the daily lives and power dynamics of the Caledonian tribes. We will also consider why the Romans eventually retreated and how their departure affected the land north of Hadrian's Wall.

---

2. Early Roman Campaigns in Britain and the Road to Caledonia

The Roman conquest of Britain started in earnest under Emperor Claudius in 43 CE. Over the next few decades, Roman legions pushed northward, overcoming various British tribes. By the late 70s CE, they were looking beyond the modern border of England into the lands of the tribes of southern Scotland. The Romans had heard stories of formidable warriors living in the mountainous and forested territory further north, and some generals were eager to conquer the entire island.

One of the earliest and most noted figures in this push was Gnaeus Julius Agricola, appointed Governor of Britain in 77 CE. Under his leadership, Roman legions marched north into what is now southern Scotland. Agricola intended to extend Roman power, secure borders, and possibly tap into new resources. He also wanted to curb the threat of raids that sometimes spilled southward. Roman discipline, organization, and advanced weaponry gave them an advantage over many smaller tribal forces. Yet Caledonia's rugged landscapes, variable weather, and fierce local resistance would soon test the legions' resolve.

3. Agricola's Campaigns and the Battle of Mons Graupius

Agricola spent several years campaigning in northern Britain, building forts and establishing supply lines. His most famous clash with the Caledonian tribes occurred around 83 CE, when he led his forces deep into the Highlands. The Roman historian Tacitus, Agricola's son-in-law, wrote an account of these events, focusing on a major battle he called Mons Graupius. The exact location of this battlefield is still debated, but many believe it was somewhere in northeast Scotland.

Tacitus claimed that thousands of Caledonians fell in the fight, while Roman casualties were comparatively low. According to the Roman narrative, the Caledonians attacked in a courageous but disorganized manner, facing disciplined legionnaires and auxiliary troops with superior training. However, we must note that Tacitus's account may be exaggerated or biased. He aimed to glorify Agricola's achievements and emphasize Roman superiority. Realistically, the tribes might have retreated into the more remote areas, using guerrilla tactics that made a definitive Roman victory difficult to sustain.

Even if Mons Graupius was a Roman success, it did not result in total conquest of Caledonia. Shortly after this campaign, Agricola was recalled to Rome. The legions did not maintain the same momentum. The Roman Empire had priorities elsewhere, and the cost of holding the far north seemed high compared to the potential benefits. Still, Agricola's campaigns proved that Roman forces could at least temporarily march throughout much of Caledonia. They built roads, camps, and forts to house troops.

These structures became the stepping stones for continued Roman presence in southern Scotland.

4. Establishing and Abandoning the Northern Frontier

In the years following Agricola's governorship, Roman control in the north fluctuated. Emperors and governors changed policy based on shifting threats and resources. Sometimes they tried to hold territory beyond the River Forth, but at other times, they pulled back to more defendable lines. One of the major developments came in 122 CE, when Emperor Hadrian visited Britain. He ordered the construction of a fortification across northern England to mark Rome's permanent frontier in Britain: Hadrian's Wall.

Stretching roughly from the River Tyne in the east to the Solway Firth in the west, Hadrian's Wall stood around 73 miles long. It included forts, milecastles, and turrets for surveillance. This massive building project was intended to control movement between Roman-occupied lands to the south and tribal lands to the north. It also served as a statement of power. While this wall lies outside modern Scottish borders, it influenced life in southern Scotland by shaping trade routes, limiting large-scale tribal raids, and encouraging local leaders to negotiate or cooperate with the Romans.

Later, under Emperor Antoninus Pius, around 142 CE, the Romans advanced again into southern Scotland. They built the Antonine Wall between the Firth of Forth and the Firth of Clyde. Shorter than Hadrian's Wall, it was mainly made of turf ramparts on stone foundations, with forts and fortlets along its length. The Antonine Wall showed that Rome still hoped to push its frontier further north. However, this wall was held for only a couple of decades before the legions withdrew once more to Hadrian's Wall. The pullback signaled the Empire's ongoing struggle to justify the costs of fortifying a region where control was difficult to maintain.

5. Forts, Roads, and Daily Life Under Roman Presence

Even if the Romans did not hold onto the whole of Caledonia, they left a lasting legacy in the territories they did occupy. Forts such as Trimontium (near modern Melrose), Inveresk (east of Edinburgh), and Ardoch in Perthshire testify to the Roman attempt to establish control and monitor local tribes. These forts housed soldiers and sometimes families, traders, and support staff. Inside, the Romans introduced amenities not common among local Iron Age communities, like bathhouses, granaries, and paved streets.

Roman engineers also built roads to connect forts and allow quick movement of troops. Parts of these old roads are still traceable in the modern landscape. They facilitated trade in goods like grain, cattle, hides, and even slaves. Local tribes would sometimes supply the Roman garrisons in exchange for Roman imports, such as pottery, glassware, and metal goods. This exchange introduced new items and customs to local elites, who might display Roman bronzeware or tableware at feasts to show status.

Daily life for native people living near forts or within zones of Roman influence could vary. Some Caledonians might have benefited from trade and the protection against rival tribes. Others resented the Roman demands for food and supplies, or taxes imposed by local leaders who acted as go-betweens. There is evidence of intermarriage between Roman soldiers and local women, producing children who blended both cultures. Over time, certain families became Romanized, adopting aspects of Roman dress, language (Latin), and lifestyle, while others remained more traditional, preserving local dialects and customs.

---

6. Resistance, Raids, and Tribal Alliances

Roman records speak of ongoing troubles with the northern tribes—often labeled collectively as "Caledonii," though there were many distinct groups. Even during periods of relative calm, border skirmishes or raids were common. Tribes might unite briefly against a common enemy but then break apart. The fierce reputation of these northern warriors, combined with the difficulties of sending reinforcements from the south, made it hard for Rome to fully stabilize the frontier.

Archaeological evidence shows that some hillforts were refortified around this time, suggesting that tribes invested in local defense. Some groups formed alliances, possibly seeking to share resources and coordinate tactics against Roman incursions. Others might have seen the benefit in working with the Empire, gaining trade connections or recognition from Roman authorities in exchange for keeping the peace. This patchwork of alliances and conflicts shaped the century following the building of Hadrian's and Antonine Walls.

7. The Role of Client Kingdoms and Diplomacy

Instead of direct military occupation everywhere, Roman policy in Britain and along the frontiers often involved creating "client kingdoms." These were local territories led by chieftains or kings who agreed to keep order and collect taxes on Rome's behalf. In return, they might receive Roman backing against tribal rivals. While we do not have a clear list of formal client states in Caledonia, there is evidence that some local leaders were influenced by Roman coinage, gifts, or prestige items.

Diplomacy could be as effective as force. A tribal leader who accepted Roman customs and trade could grow rich and powerful, overshadowing other chiefs who did not. However, this cooperation had limits. If the tribes felt exploited or if Roman demands grew too large, they could rebel. The scattered evidence from inscriptions, coins, and archaeology shows a mixed pattern: pockets of Roman influence alongside areas that remained mostly outside Roman control. This blend of diplomacy, trade, and intermittent warfare meant that Rome's northern frontier was not a simple dividing line but rather a zone of complex relationships.

8. Further Campaigns and Setbacks: The Severan Expedition

In the late 2nd and early 3rd centuries, Rome faced new challenges. Changes in leadership, pressures on other frontiers, and unrest in Britain itself drew imperial attention once again to the north. One of the major events was Emperor Septimius Severus's campaign in Caledonia around 208–211 CE. He led a large army to reassert Roman power, hoping to settle the frontier issue once and for all.

Severus's armies marched north of Hadrian's Wall, building or repairing forts, and confronting local tribes. However, the harsh terrain, wet climate, and guerrilla tactics of the northern warriors took a heavy toll on Roman forces. Ancient sources tell us Severus suffered enormous casualties, although the numbers might be exaggerated. The Emperor himself grew ill and died in 211 CE at Eboracum (modern York), effectively ending the campaign. His successor, Caracalla, quickly ended hostilities in the north, and no lasting conquest was achieved.

This unsuccessful attempt to dominate Caledonia underlined an ongoing theme: the region was costly, difficult to hold, and presented limited economic gain for Rome compared to other provinces. After Severus, the Empire took a more defensive stance in Britain, maintaining Hadrian's Wall as the principal border. The Antonine Wall was never fully reoccupied on a permanent basis. Any illusions of pushing the Roman frontier all the way north to the Highlands faded with Severus's death.

---

9. Economic and Cultural Influences

Though Rome never ruled all of Caledonia, regions under or near Roman control saw economic and cultural influences. Coins circulated more widely, and local craftspeople began to imitate Roman pottery, metal goods, and other items. Archaeological digs show that, in some settlements, people adapted Roman architectural features, like rectangular stone foundations or tile roofs, especially near the southern frontier zones.

Latin may have been used in official capacities or among traders, although it never replaced local languages. Over time, a hybrid material culture emerged in border communities, blending Celtic and Roman elements. Traders or traveling craftspeople carried new designs and techniques further inland, even where Roman governance did not extend. This is why, for example, some Iron Age jewelry from northern Scotland shows stylistic influences that can be traced back to Roman Britain.

Additionally, the Roman love of wine, olive oil, and exotic spices left traces. Amphora fragments—large pottery vessels for transporting wine or oil—have been found at some Scottish sites. These were usually associated with elite households or garrisons that could afford such luxuries. Although these imported items were never common for the general population, they highlight how far goods could travel along Rome's vast trade networks.

10. Withdrawal of Roman Authority and Its Consequences

By the early 4th century, Rome's grip on Britain overall was weakening. Threats from continental invasions, internal power struggles, and economic strain forced the Empire to pull resources away from its western provinces. In the early 5th century, Roman administrators and legions largely withdrew from Britain, leaving local communities to fend for themselves. While this departure is often dated to 410 CE (when Emperor Honorius supposedly told Britons to look to their own defense), the process was gradual.

In what is now southern Scotland, the forts fell into disuse. Some might have been taken over by local warlords or abandoned entirely. Hadrian's Wall was no longer maintained, although local populations might have reused the stones for their own buildings. Without a central authority, smaller kingdoms and tribal federations emerged. The "Romanized" elites who had depended on imperial support either adapted to new conditions or lost power. Trade networks that relied on a stable Roman market declined, forcing local economies to become more self-reliant.

North of Hadrian's Wall, tribes continued as they had, though the departure of Roman troops changed the balance of power among different groups. Some took advantage of the vacuum to expand their territory or renew old rivalries. The legacy of Roman influence did not vanish, however. Roman roads, forts, and bits of material culture remained in the landscape. Over time, the memory of Roman power turned into legend, influencing later stories of a once-mighty empire that built massive walls and roads across Britain.

---

11. Legacy and Long-Term Effects in Caledonia

Although Rome never fully conquered Scotland, its presence left lasting imprints:

1. **Frontier Walls and Forts**
   - Hadrian's Wall, while south of the modern border, shaped the cultural and economic exchanges with the region we now call Scotland.
   - The Antonine Wall, though short-lived, showed Rome's ambition to control southern Scotland and remains a physical reminder of their reach.
2. **Road Networks**
   - Roman roads provided routes that would be reused in medieval and modern times, aiding travel and trade well after Rome's departure.
3. **Economic and Cultural Exchange**
   - Goods like pottery, glass, and coins trickled into Caledonia, encouraging some local artisans to adopt new styles or techniques.
   - A partial Romanization of local elites took place, though it was limited and never absolute.
4. **Military Experience**
   - The tribes gained knowledge of Roman tactics, siege technologies, and weaponry through both war and cooperation, possibly influencing their own military practices.
5. **Shift in Power Structures**

- The presence of Rome prompted the rise of client leaders and new tribal alliances. After Rome left, these alliances evolved into post-Roman kingdoms and confederations.

This layered impact means that when we look at the centuries after Roman withdrawal, we can still see hints of Roman influence in language borrowings, place names near old forts, and even in the spread of Christianity, which sometimes traveled along former Roman roads or garrison routes.

12. Transition to the Next Chapter: Enter the Picts

Once the Roman Empire departed, the power vacuum left behind led to significant changes. Tribal groups in the north, many of whom were labeled "Picti" by Roman writers, became more prominent. They were known for raids south of the frontier, but they also developed their own kingdoms and a strong cultural identity. We do not have clear records from the Picts themselves, but archaeological evidence and later sources paint a picture of a unique people with distinctive art, symbols, and social structures.

In our next chapter, we will move from the fading shadow of the Roman presence into the era when the Picts took center stage in northern Britain. As we discuss these "painted" or "tattooed" people, we will see how they formed powerful kingdoms, adapted to changing times, and built a legacy that would influence the shape of Scotland. Though the Roman chapter of Caledonia's history was relatively brief, it set the stage for new developments, including the emergence of the Pictish kingdoms.

CHAPTER 4

THE AGE OF THE PICTS

1. Introduction

With the Romans gone or limited to the fringes, the groups who inhabited northern Britain during the late 3rd to 9th centuries became more visible in the historical record. Chief among them were the Picts, a confederation of tribes who occupied much of what is now eastern and northern Scotland. The term "Picti," meaning "painted people," first appeared in Roman writings, possibly referring to body art or tattoos. Over time, this label stuck, although we do not know what the Picts called themselves.

During the Age of the Picts, the region saw the formation of small kingdoms, the growth of stone carving traditions, and the spread of Christianity. The Picts defended their lands against external threats—first against remaining Roman forces, then against incursions by Angles from the south and Vikings from the north. They also interacted with Gaelic settlers from Ireland, who would eventually form the Kingdom of Dalriada. This chapter will take an in-depth look at the Picts: their origins, society, art, religion, and eventual transformation into what later evolved into the medieval Kingdom of Alba.

---

2. The Origins of the Picts

The exact origins of the Picts are complex. They likely descended from Iron Age tribes who lived in eastern and northern Scotland. As Roman power declined, these tribes may have formed alliances or confederations to protect themselves and assert their independence. Roman authors of the 3rd century mention groups north of Hadrian's Wall collectively, sometimes calling them "Caledonians" or "Picti." Over time, "Pict" became a more common term in external writings.

A few scattered references hint that the Picts were not a single unified kingdom at first. Instead, they comprised multiple groups, each with its own chief or king. They may have shared common cultural traits, such as language or body art, which led outsiders to group them under one name. Early on, Pictish raiders ventured south, attacking Roman frontier zones or crossing the sea to raid communities in Britain and Ireland. These raids contributed to the Picts' fearsome reputation among neighboring peoples.

The language of the Picts is still debated. Some scholars think it was a Brythonic Celtic tongue, related to Welsh and Cumbric. Others propose that it might have included non-Indo-European elements. Unfortunately, the Picts left no extensive written records in their own language, so we rely on place names, personal names, and carved symbols to glean clues. Whatever their linguistic or ethnic roots, the Picts developed a distinct identity that set them apart from the Britons to the south, the Gaels to the west, and the later Norse settlers in the north.

---

3. Early Pictish Kingdoms and Power Centers

By the 6th century, the Pictish world was made up of several key regions, often referred to as kingdoms or provinces. Among them were Fortriu (possibly centered around Moray and the north-east), Fib (modern Fife), Circinn (near Angus), and others. Each kingdom likely had its own ruler, who might claim authority over smaller local chiefs. The concept of kingship was important. Rulers needed both military success and ritual legitimacy, which might include Christian anointing once the faith spread, or older forms of inauguration that involved sacred sites.

Archaeological evidence for these early kingdoms comes from hillforts and strongholds, often placed in strategic locations. One major Pictish center might have been at Burghead in Moray, featuring substantial walls and a seaward outlook. Another could be found at Craig Phadrig near Inverness. These fortified sites often included large timber or stone halls where feasts, gatherings, or councils took place. Wealth, in the form of cattle, slaves, or precious metal objects, played a big role in asserting power. Kings who secured alliances through marriage or exchanged hostages with neighboring rulers could build broader support, strengthening their claim over a region.

Competition between these Pictish kingdoms was common. Warfare did not necessarily involve large-scale armies, but rather bands of warriors under local chiefs. Raiding was a recognized method of building prestige, as long as it was successful. Periods of unity might occur when a particularly strong king overcame rivals to become the "King of the Picts." But that unity was often fragile, especially when a king died, triggering disputes over succession. Over time, these internal dynamics shaped the shifting map of Pictish power and set the stage for interactions with external groups, such as the Gaels and Anglo-Saxons.

---

4. The Spread of Christianity among the Picts

Christianity began to penetrate Pictish territories through various channels. One route was from the south, via former Roman Christian communities in Britain. Another significant route was from the west, through Irish missionaries and monastic foundations. By the 5th and 6th centuries, figures like St. Ninian and St. Columba became central to the Christian mission among the Picts. Tradition says St. Ninian established a church at Whithorn in Galloway, influencing areas that might have had contact with the southern Picts. However, solid historical evidence for Ninian's activities is limited.

St. Columba's work is better documented. Columba was an Irish monk who founded the monastery of Iona around 563 CE, off the western coast of Scotland. While Columba mainly worked among the Gaels of Dalriada, he also traveled north and east, meeting Pictish kings. One legend says he visited the court of King Bridei (also spelled Brude), who ruled the powerful kingdom of Fortriu from his fortress near Inverness. Through preaching, miracles, and forging relationships with local elites, Columba and his successors established monasteries in Pictish lands. Over the generations, many Picts were baptized, and Christian practices took root.

Christianity brought new cultural elements—Latin literacy, church organization, and connections to Ireland and continental Europe.

Monasteries functioned as centers of learning, script production, and artistic patronage. They also provided a platform for local leaders to link themselves with the broader Christian community, which could raise their status. As Christian institutions gained influence, certain older religious practices or beliefs may have merged with new teachings, creating a blend of Christian and local traditions in Pictish society.

---

5. Pictish Art and Symbol Stones

One of the most distinctive legacies of the Picts is their stone carving. Across eastern and northern Scotland, standing stones bear carved symbols, figures, and later, Christian crosses. These "Pictish symbol stones" are categorized into several classes, each reflecting different styles or time periods. Early stones (Class I) often feature incised symbols—like the crescent and V-rod, double disc and Z-rod, and animals like the Pictish beast. Later stones (Class II) add Christian crosses and more elaborate designs, sometimes in high relief. Class III stones show further evolution of style, often dominated by Christian iconography and more naturalistic figures.

The meaning of the symbols on these stones is still debated. They might denote clan identities, commemorate important individuals, or mark territorial boundaries. Some could hold religious or mythological significance. The distribution of certain symbols in particular areas suggests local traditions, while others appear widely, hinting at shared cultural practices across Pictland. The presence of crosses on many later stones shows how Christianity merged with native artistic expression.

In addition to symbol stones, the Picts created remarkable decorative metalwork, including brooches and ornate objects for both secular and religious use. Though not as well preserved as the stones, metal finds confirm that the Picts had skilled artisans who adopted and adapted styles from Celtic, Anglo-Saxon, and other artistic traditions. These crafts highlight the interplay between local culture and wider influences, demonstrating that the Picts were far from isolated.

6. Interaction with the Gaels and the Kingdom of Dalriada

While the Picts dominated eastern and northern regions, Gaelic-speaking settlers from Ireland had established themselves in the west, forming the Kingdom of Dalriada. The Gaels, also known as the Scoti, brought their own language (Old Gaelic) and cultural practices. Over time, Dalriada expanded, forging ties with Christian monasteries like Iona. As the Gaels strengthened their position, they occasionally clashed with Pictish neighbors.

However, war was not the only form of interaction. Marriages between Pictish and Gaelic royal families helped create alliances. Trade routes connected communities across the Highlands, sharing goods like cattle, hides, or precious metals. Monastic networks fostered religious and cultural exchange. While the Picts and Gaels maintained distinct identities, their proximity and shared Christian faith led to a degree of overlap in art, burial practices, and possibly even language borrowings.

One of the key outcomes of these interactions was the gradual shift of power in northern Britain. By the 8th and 9th centuries, the Gaels of Dalriada began to merge with or overshadow certain Pictish territories. This slow process involved political maneuvering, military might, and the complex lineage ties of royal families. Much later, chroniclers claimed that Kenneth MacAlpin (Cináed mac Ailpín) united the Picts and Gaels in the mid-9th century, laying the foundation for the Kingdom of Alba. While the exact details remain murky, it is clear that Gaelic influence grew stronger over time, transforming the region's political landscape.

---

7. Conflict with the Angles and Other Neighbors

The Picts also faced threats from the south and east. As the Roman Empire's presence faded, new groups moved into northern Britain. The Angles, who formed the kingdom of Bernicia (later part of Northumbria), expanded their territory up to the River Forth. They built fortresses and established a powerful presence in Lothian. This brought them into direct conflict with Pictish kingdoms in the southeast. Battles, shifting alliances, and occasional truces defined the relations between the Picts and Northumbrians.

A notable clash occurred at the Battle of Dun Nechtain (also called Nechtansmere) in 685 CE. King Bridei III of the Picts defeated the forces of King Ecgfrith of Northumbria in a major confrontation. This victory halted Northumbrian expansion into Pictish lands and restored Pictish confidence. The battle is often seen as a key turning point, securing Pictish independence for several generations. It also had broader implications for the political balance in northern Britain, reinforcing the idea that the Pictish kingdoms were far from weak.

Meanwhile, the Britons of Strathclyde to the southwest and the Gaelic kingdom of Dalriada to the west provided other potential allies or enemies. The Picts often tried to maintain a balance of power, forging alliances against a common foe or raiding when opportunity arose. The resulting political map was fluid, with shifting lines of control. Over centuries, the Picts proved they could stand against powerful neighbors like Northumbria, even if their alliances and internal unity were often fragile.

---

8. Viking Raids and Pressures

Starting in the late 8th century, Norse Vikings began to raid the coasts of Scotland, targeting monasteries and wealthy settlements. Iona was attacked multiple times, along with other Christian centers. The Picts were vulnerable to seaborne raids along the north and east coasts, where many of their key power centers were located. The Vikings plundered local wealth, disrupted trade, and sometimes settled in parts of the northern islands, including Orkney and Shetland.

Viking aggression forced Pictish leaders to shift resources to coastal defense. Some areas, especially the northern isles and parts of the Hebrides, fell under Norse control. This introduced new political dynamics, as local chiefs had to either negotiate with Vikings or flee inland. Over time, the Norse established earldoms, integrating with the local population in certain regions. The direct pressure from Viking raids weakened some

Pictish kingdoms, making them more susceptible to Gaelic expansion or internal strife.

Despite these challenges, the Picts continued to resist Norse incursions where possible. On the mainland, fortified centers and alliances helped repel large-scale invasions, though short-term raids remained a threat. As the Viking Age progressed, the mosaic of power in northern Britain became even more complex. Gaels, Picts, and Norse groups all vied for territory, trading opportunities, and influence. In the end, these pressures contributed to a gradual realignment of power that would shape the early medieval period in Scotland.

---

9. Society, Family, and Law in Pictland

While political and military events often grab our attention, daily life in Pictland also underwent important changes. The Picts lived in small farming communities, as well as in or around royal strongholds. They raised cattle, sheep, and pigs; grew barley and oats; and fished rivers and seas. Craftspeople produced pottery, textiles, and metal items. As Christianity spread, monasteries and churches became centers not only of worship but also of learning and local economy.

Family structures in Pictland are thought by some historians to have included matrilineal aspects, where royal succession could pass through the mother's line. However, this theory is still debated. It is possible that both paternal and maternal lines were considered for kingship, or that local customs varied. What is clear is that Pictish law placed great importance on kinship and alliances by marriage. Conflict resolution could involve compensation payments, known in some Celtic societies as "blood fines." Church leaders might arbitrate disputes, reflecting the growing authority of Christian clergy.

Social stratification existed, with kings, nobles, and warriors holding higher status. Monasteries added another layer of influence, with abbots sometimes challenging royal power. Common farmers, craftspeople, and slaves (often captured in raids) formed the bulk of the population. Over time, the spread of literacy through the Church created a small educated class capable of recording genealogies, religious texts, and possibly laws, though much has been lost.

10. The Decline and Transformation of the Pictish Identity

By the 9th century, the political landscape shifted dramatically. Repeated Viking attacks destabilized coastal regions, while Gaelic rulers in the west gained strength. Intermarriage between Pictish and Gaelic royal families blurred ethnic lines at the highest levels of society. As Gaelic became more prominent in royal courts, Pictish language and customs merged with Gaelic practices. Some historians place great emphasis on the reign of Kenneth MacAlpin (mid-9th century), who is traditionally credited with bringing Pictish and Gaelic crowns together. Whether this event was a single conquest, a negotiated union, or a gradual process is debated. Nonetheless, it marked a turning point.

Over time, the term "Pict" faded from the historical record, replaced by references to the kingdom of Alba and its Gaelic-speaking rulers. By the 10th century, many major references to the Picts vanish, suggesting that Pictish identity was either absorbed or rebranded under Gaelic dominance. The physical remnants—symbol stones, hillforts, and churches—remained as silent witnesses to a once-distinct cultural group. And so the Age of the Picts transitioned into the early medieval kingdom that would eventually evolve into Scotland.

11. Legacy of the Picts

Although the Picts as a named people disappeared from the written record, their influence persisted in several ways:

1. **Artistic Heritage**
    - The symbol stones and decorative metalwork left behind continue to fascinate archaeologists, historians, and art lovers.

- Pictish motifs and styles may have influenced later Scottish art forms, especially in stone carving and manuscript illumination.
2. **Religious Developments**
    - The Christian foundations established among the Picts helped shape the monastic tradition that later became part of the broader Church in Scotland.
    - Several churches and monasteries traced their origins to Pictish patronage, maintaining local devotions that survived political upheavals.
3. **Place Names**
    - Many place names in eastern and northern Scotland may have Pictish roots, even if adapted later into Gaelic or Scots.
    - Certain linguistic elements still puzzle scholars, hinting at a hidden layer of Pictish influence on modern Scottish geography.
4. **Political Foundations**
    - The merging of Pictish and Gaelic leadership set the groundwork for the kingdom of Alba, which expanded and eventually took on the name "Scotland."
    - Legends of Pictish kings and heroes lingered in medieval chronicles, shaping Scottish identity and lore in subtle ways.
5. **Cultural Mystique**
    - Because the Picts left limited written records, their story retains an air of mystery. Modern researchers continue to debate the meanings of Pictish symbols and the exact nature of their language.
    - This mystery has fueled romantic and nationalistic interpretations, making the Picts a topic of ongoing fascination.

---

12. Transition to Future Chapters

The Age of the Picts saw significant social, religious, and political developments in northern Britain. They built a distinctive culture, resisted powerful neighbors, and eventually fused with Gaelic peoples to form the foundation of the medieval Kingdom of Alba. As we move forward in this book, we will see how other groups—Gaels, Vikings, Normans—further shaped the land and culture of Scotland. But the Pictish chapter remains vital to understanding Scotland's early medieval roots.

In the coming chapters, we will look at the arrival of the Gaels more closely and the creation of Dalriada, followed by the formation of a unified kingdom under rulers who drew from both Pictish and Gaelic traditions. This will carry us into the Viking Age, the emergence of Alba, and the eventual shaping of medieval Scotland.

CHAPTER 5

THE ARRIVAL OF THE GAELS AND THE KINGDOM OF DALRIADA

1. Introduction

By the end of the Pictish era as an independent force, another group of people had taken root on the western shores of what we now call Scotland: the Gaels. Referred to by some as "Scoti," these Gaelic-speaking settlers originally crossed the sea from Ireland (then called "Hibernia") and established footholds along the coast of Argyll and surrounding islands. Over time, these settlers formed a kingdom known as Dalriada, or Dál Riata in Gaelic. Although small at first, this kingdom grew in power. Its people farmed, fished, traded, and, eventually, shaped the future of all Scotland.

This chapter will explore the background of these Gaelic settlers, how they arrived, and how they created Dalriada. We will look at their social structures, warfare, religious practices, and interactions with neighboring peoples. In doing so, we see how Gaelic influence slowly intertwined with Pictish tradition, planting the seeds for a larger kingdom. By the chapter's end, we will understand how the Gaels from Ireland left a deep imprint on Scottish culture, language, and political life—an influence that would grow even stronger in the centuries ahead.

---

2. Gaelic Origins and Early Movements

The Gaels (or Scoti) who arrived in western Scotland were part of a broader migration and cultural connection spanning the Irish Sea. Ireland's earliest historical sources speak of tribal groups, each ruled by chieftains who often competed for power. Over time, some adventurous families or smaller tribal branches looked outward, seeking new pastures or opportunities in Britain. The southwestern region of Argyll, with its rugged shoreline, numerous inlets, and islands, was geographically close to northeastern Ireland and likely attractive for settling.

Seafaring was crucial to Gaelic expansion. Although basic by modern standards, the wooden boats of early Gaels were sturdy enough for short sea crossings. Cargo, livestock, and families could be ferried across the narrow channel between northeastern Ireland and Kintyre. Over generations, a Gaelic-speaking community took hold, sustained by fishing, coastal farming, and trade. Small Gaelic enclaves developed, forming the nucleus of what would become Dalriada. While precise dates are hard to pin down, many scholars place the core Gaelic settlement in Argyll by the 5th century CE or earlier.

In Ireland itself, rival clans frequently fought for territory. Some Gaelic families might have ventured across the sea to escape conflict, while others did so in pursuit of wealth, freedom, or alliances with existing Brittonic or Pictish groups. These Gaels brought their language, traditions, and leadership structures, which would adapt over time to the local environment of the western Scottish coast.

---

3. Landscape, Resources, and Early Settlements

Argyll's landscape shaped the newcomers' way of life. Long sea lochs carved deep into the mainland, providing sheltered harbors where small boats could land. Nearby, the rolling hills and glens, though rocky in places, offered pasture for cattle and sheep. The Gaels farmed barley and oats in coastal areas, supplementing their diet with fish, shellfish, and wild game. These resources could sustain small communities, even if yields were sometimes modest due to the challenging climate and terrain.

Settlements were typically small clusters of roundhouses or rectangular wooden buildings. Over time, local materials—stone, timber, and thatch—were used in construction. In some coastal areas, promontory forts or duns were built to protect strategic headlands. Similar to Iron Age structures, these forts featured earthworks and stone ramparts. They served as refuges during raids or places where chieftains might display their status. As the Gaelic population grew, certain families or clans rose in prominence, gathering followers and forging alliances with kin back in Ireland.

Trade routes across the Irish Sea connected Gaelic communities on both sides. People shared tools, livestock, metalwork, and news. Marriages across the water strengthened bonds, tying Argyll closer to its Irish roots. While local differences emerged—such as building styles or certain farming techniques—the Gaels in Scotland recognized their cultural links with Ireland, maintaining a sense of shared heritage.

---

4. Emergence of the Kingdom of Dalriada

The scattered Gaelic settlements in Argyll eventually coalesced under a ruling dynasty, leading to what became known as the Kingdom of Dalriada. The exact process remains uncertain, but references in early medieval Irish annals suggest that a Gaelic leader, possibly named Fergus Mór mac Eirc, played a key role in unifying smaller groups during the 5th or 6th century. Whether he was the single founder or merely one of several influential kings is debated, but Fergus Mór became emblematic of the Gaelic establishment in Argyll.

Dalriada likely began as a patchwork of kin-based territories called "tuatha." Over time, a dominant lineage secured leadership over these tuatha, forging a larger entity. Strategic marriages, alliances with influential Irish families, and success in battle all played roles in consolidating power. Once the kingdom emerged, its heartland included Kintyre, Lorn, Islay, and neighboring islands. Rulers often resided near coastal strongholds or on islands like Dunadd, a rocky outcrop in modern Argyll that would become a ceremonial center for Gaelic kings.

From Dunadd and other bases, Dalriadan kings worked to strengthen their domain. They levied tribute, regulated trade, and maintained local defenses. Yet Dalriada's authority was not absolute. Clans within the kingdom preserved their own customs, lands, and loyalties, requiring the king to skillfully balance local interests. Over time, the Dalriadan leadership extended influence beyond Argyll, engaging with Pictish neighbors to the east. Such expansion efforts sometimes sparked conflict, but they also opened doors to alliances and cultural exchange.

5. Gaelic Society: Clans, Kinship, and Kingship

Central to Gaelic life was the concept of kinship. Families traced descent through paternal lineages, forming clans or extended households. Within these groups, loyalty was essential. Resources like land and livestock were commonly controlled at a kin group level, and disputes were often resolved through compensation or mediation by elders. The Gaelic language helped bind communities together, reinforcing shared tales, oral law codes, and genealogies that preserved clan identities.

Kingship in Dalriada was similarly bound up with kinship principles. A king, or "rí," was typically chosen from a royal lineage, but not strictly by primogeniture. Instead, various male relatives in the royal house might contend for the throne. This system, called "tanistry," could spark power struggles, especially when multiple candidates claimed legitimacy. Yet it also kept the pool of potential leaders broad, preventing a single family branch from monopolizing power for too long.

Under Dalriada's kings, society was stratified into nobles, common freemen, and unfree people (slaves or bonded laborers). Nobles owned larger herds and controlled strategic land. They served as the king's subordinates, providing warriors during times of war. Freemen farmed small plots or joined communal herding. Slaves were often war captives or debt slaves. The entire social fabric was supported by agricultural production, herding, and intermittent raiding. Wealth was measured in cattle, an important currency in Gaelic society. Kings used feasts, gift-giving, and the spoils of raids to maintain loyalty among nobles and warriors.

---

6. Warfare, Raids, and Rivalries

Gaelic warfare in early Dalriada often revolved around small-scale raids, feuds between clans, or conflicts with neighboring territories. These engagements rarely resembled massive pitched battles; instead, groups of warriors might strike quickly, seizing livestock, plunder, or hostages. The Gaelic word for such raiding, "crech," reflects a long-standing cultural acceptance of raids as a means to display bravery, gain wealth, and avenge insults. However, large-scale confrontations also occurred, especially when powerful kings attempted to unify or expand territory.

Weapons included spears, swords, bows, and shields. Armor was limited, often just leather or thick wool tunics. Leaders might carry ornate weapons or wear precious ornaments to signal status. Poets or "filí" occasionally accompanied warriors, composing verses that celebrated heroic deeds and kept genealogies. These warrior-poets held special esteem in Gaelic culture, praising or criticizing kings according to their actions in battle or how well they honored guests.

Beyond internal strife, Dalriada faced external threats. Pictish rulers to the north and east might contest borderlands, while the Britons of Strathclyde in the south sometimes clashed with Gaelic forces in southwestern areas. Across the Irish Sea, rival clans from Ireland could attempt to reassert influence or raid Gaelic-settled lands in Scotland. Such rivalries and military pressures shaped the kingdom's political landscape, forging alliances, marriages, and treaties meant to stabilize Dalriada's position.

---

7. The Influence of Christianity in Dalriada

Christianity played a key role in uniting Gaelic communities and connecting Dalriada with the broader Christian world. Missionaries and monks from Ireland had already spread the faith widely there, establishing monastic sites that served as centers of worship, education, and art. As Gaels moved to Argyll, they brought Christian practices along. By the 6th century, a monastic network began to flourish in Dalriada as well, with direct ties to the famous Irish monastic tradition.

One of the most significant influences came from St. Columba, who settled on the island of Iona in 563 CE. Although this monastery primarily served the Gaelic kingdom in the west, its reach extended across northern Britain, including Pictish territories. Iona became a hub for religious learning, manuscript production, and missionary work. The abbots there often advised Gaelic kings, traveling to royal courts to mediate disputes or oversee important ceremonies. Kings who were favored by the Church could claim divine sanction for their rule, strengthening their legitimacy.

Monasteries in Dalriada collected tithes, welcomed pilgrims, and provided social services. They also produced intricate art, exemplified by illuminated manuscripts and carved stone crosses. Gaelic scribes adapted symbols and decorative elements from older Celtic traditions, blending them with Christian themes. These sacred centers thus reinforced both religious devotion and a shared Gaelic identity. As monastic communities spread, they helped shape moral and legal norms, sometimes offering an alternative to feuding by encouraging peace treaties and arbitration. In many ways, the Church acted as a stabilizing force in an otherwise fractious political environment.

---

8. Cultural Exchange with the Picts

Though conflict between Dalriada and the Picts was frequent, there were also periods of peace and cultural exchange. Trade routes linked coastal communities in southwestern Dalriada to eastern Pictish territories through rivers and overland tracks. Salted fish, hides, and perhaps even small amounts of precious metals could have changed hands. Christian monks traversed these routes as well, establishing or supporting churches across cultural boundaries. Monastic centers sometimes fell under both Gaelic and Pictish patronage.

Intermarriage between royal families also acted as a bridge. A Gaelic king might wed a Pictish princess, or vice versa, securing an alliance that reduced hostilities. Through such unions, Gaelic language and customs gradually spread eastward, while Pictish styles in art or architecture seeped into Gaelic lands. In places, we see a mixture of Pictish symbol stone tradition and Gaelic cross-carving, suggesting a deepening blend of influences. Though each side maintained distinct identities, the push and pull of war, trade, and marriage wove them closer together over time.

An example of shared culture can be seen in certain religious dedications. Churches that started as Gaelic monastic outposts might later gain Pictish benefactors, or adopt local saints. Conversely, Pictish devotion to a particular holy figure sometimes spread into Gaelic Argyll. This spiritual overlap helped soften boundaries, preparing the way for broader unification movements that would emerge in later centuries.

9. Dalriada's Shifting Fortunes

Dalriada's power and extent varied over time, influenced by internal leadership struggles and external pressures. Some kings achieved significant consolidation, launching raids against Pictish neighbors or even into British territories to the south. These campaigns could yield cattle, slaves, and prestige. However, setbacks were also frequent. A lost battle or a particularly harsh winter might weaken royal authority, emboldening rival clans or encouraging Picts to counterattack.

The kingdom's fortunes were also tied to events in Ireland. If a Dalriadan king maintained strong ties with influential Irish kin, he might receive military or diplomatic support. Conversely, if an Irish branch of the royal house faced upheaval, it could leave the Scottish branch more isolated. The sea routes that had once fostered Gaelic migration also provided pathways for enemies or disgruntled relatives to invade. As a result, Dalriada's expansion in one generation could be reversed in the next, forcing kings to constantly reaffirm their dominance through warfare and strategic marriages.

We see hints of such patterns in early medieval annals, which record the names of Dalriadan kings, their battles, and their alliances. Most references are terse, giving only a glimpse of the swirling politics. Even so, these sources confirm that Dalriada was an active player in the power dynamics of northern Britain—a kingdom that could punch above its weight at times but was never entirely secure.

10. Social and Economic Structures

Beneath the royal courts and warrior elites, the backbone of Dalriadan society was its agricultural community. Gaelic farmers worked small plots, tending grains that could survive in the cool, wet climate. They raised cattle, which formed a principal measure of wealth and were integral to both feasts and religious offerings. Sheep provided wool for clothing, while pigs foraged in woodlands. Fishing supplemented the food supply in coastal areas. Thanks to these resources, Dalriada's population, though modest, had enough to sustain local markets and feasts that cemented alliances among chiefs.

Trade occurred along the coasts and across the Irish Sea. Gaelic merchants might transport woolen goods, leather, or surplus grain to Ireland in exchange for iron tools, crafted metal items, or even exotic items from farther afield. Over land, pack animals carried goods between Gaelic settlements and neighboring Pictish markets. Salt, essential for food preservation, was also a valuable trade commodity. Artistic items, such as finely worked brooches or decorative scabbards, could serve as diplomatic gifts, forging bonds between clans.

The societal hierarchy placed kings and nobles at the top, with freemen making up the majority of the farming and herding workforce. Some skilled craftsmen, such as blacksmiths, enjoyed elevated status due to the importance of their trade. The Church offered a parallel path to influence for those who became monks, priests, or abbots, although religious life often transcended direct clan loyalties. Slaves, taken as war captives or born into servitude, occupied the lowest rung. They labored in fields or households, their rights and freedoms dictated by clan-based norms and often reliant on the mercy of their masters.

---

11. Art, Language, and Oral Traditions

Dalriada left a mark on the cultural history of Scotland through its Gaelic language and rich oral traditions. Poets (filí) and storytellers performed at feasts, reciting genealogies, heroic tales, and moral stories. These performances were not just entertainment; they were a crucial means of preserving clan history and identity. Skilled poets could enhance a king's reputation or tarnish it with satirical verses. Rulers rewarded supportive poets with gifts of cattle or land, linking literary talent to power.

In material culture, the Gaels continued the Celtic legacy of intricate metalwork. While large-scale artifacts are rare, smaller finds such as brooches, bracelets, and weapon fittings show swirling, interlaced patterns reminiscent of Irish and wider Celtic art. Early Christian influences introduced crosses and biblical motifs, merging with older styles to create something distinct within Dalriada. Although the kingdom did not develop the stone monument tradition as extensively as the Picts, a few carved stones in Argyll reflect Gaelic craftsmanship and Christian devotion.

Writing in Latin script began to appear in monastic contexts, primarily for copying religious texts. Gaelic itself was mostly preserved through oral tradition during this era, though some personal names and place names show up in monastic notes or genealogical lists. Iona's scribes likely recorded significant events or wrote saints' lives that mentioned Gaelic kings, providing precious windows into Dalriada's history. Over time, these textual efforts helped lay the groundwork for the Gaelic literary tradition that would blossom in later centuries.

---

12. Relationships with Britons and Angles

Beyond dealings with the Picts, Dalriada occasionally interacted with Britons in the kingdom of Strathclyde, located to the south, and with the Angles in Northumbria, farther east. These relationships were shaped by the constantly shifting alliances of early medieval Britain. A Gaelic king might ally with Strathclyde against Pictish aggression, only to fight the Britons later if disputes arose over territory or tribute.

The Angles of Northumbria, who had expanded their power from the 7th century onward, were also a concern. Northumbria's kings sometimes intervened in western affairs, forging pacts with Dalriada or launching raids. An ambitious Gaelic king might join forces with the Picts to repel an Angle invasion, or, in other scenarios, might side with the Angles against a threatening Pictish ruler. These fluid coalitions reflect a complex geopolitical environment, where survival often hinged on tactical partnerships rather than permanent loyalties.

Despite occasional cooperation, cultural differences set Dalriada apart from both Britons and Angles. The Gaelic language and traditions had deeper connections to Ireland than to the old Roman-influenced civilization of the Britons or the Germanic heritage of the Angles. Still, monastic Christianity provided a form of common ground, with Irish missionaries playing a role in converting both Anglo-Saxon and British elites. Religious gatherings sometimes brought leaders together in relative peace, even if political tensions ran high.

13. Dalriada and Viking Incursions

Before Vikings became a major force in Scottish affairs, the Gaels of Dalriada began hearing rumors of Norse raids across the Irish Sea. By the late 8th century, Viking ships had started appearing on the coasts, targeting monasteries and settlements. Iona itself was famously attacked in the closing years of the 8th century, shocking the monastic community that had been a pillar of Dalriadan and Gaelic spirituality for generations.

Initially, the raids were sporadic, focusing on easy plunder rather than permanent occupation. Still, these attacks added a new layer of tension to Dalriada's political landscape. Kings had to fortify coastal sites, build alliances with other threatened realms, or negotiate ransoms to protect sacred centers. As Viking expeditions grew bolder, some settled on the islands, including the Hebrides and parts of the western seaboard. This new presence disrupted trade routes, sowed further chaos in local power balances, and forced Gaelic rulers to confront a foreign foe whose military prowess and mobility were formidable.

Though Vikings would come to have an even bigger role in the centuries ahead, Dalriada's encounters with them foreshadowed the broader conflicts that would reshape northern Britain. Some Gaelic warriors adapted Norse fighting styles or even formed alliances with certain Viking leaders to gain advantage over domestic rivals. However, such short-term gains risked inviting more Norse settlement, eroding Dalriada's control over key maritime routes.

14. The Road Toward Greater Unification

By the early 9th century, the lines between Pictish and Gaelic realms had blurred somewhat. Shared Christian faith, dynastic marriages, and the frequent need to form defensive alliances against external threats—whether from Northumbria or from Viking raiders—tied the two groups closer together. Some Gaelic kings might inherit Pictish titles through maternal lineage, or gain Pictish support for campaigns in return for political concessions. Meanwhile, certain Pictish rulers sought Gaelic allies to fend off hostile neighbors.

These overlapping interests helped lay the groundwork for what would eventually become a more unified realm. While each group retained its identity, the idea of a combined kingdom under a single monarch began to seem feasible, especially when facing a strong enemy. In the late 8th and early 9th centuries, Pictish weakness after repeated Viking raids offered Gaelic rulers a chance to extend influence north and east. Powerful Gaelic dynasts, with ties to both Dalriada and Pictish aristocracy, capitalized on this situation.

It is in this context that future kings like Kenneth MacAlpin would emerge, claiming both Gaelic and Pictish heritage. The story of MacAlpin, who is traditionally credited with uniting the Picts and Gaels, belongs to our next chapter. But it is clear that Dalriada's presence in Argyll set in motion the cultural and political steps that would lead to a more cohesive Scottish kingdom.

---

15. Legacy of Dalriada

Dalriada's importance in Scottish history lies in more than just battles or dynasties. The Gaelic language, carried by Dalriada's settlers and rulers, eventually spread throughout much of Scotland, influencing place names, customs, and social structures. The Gaelic Church, centered on Iona and related monastic sites, proved pivotal in shaping religious life, literacy, and art. Dalriada's kings, though often overshadowed by later medieval rulers, established the model of Gaelic kingship that blended warrior culture with Christian ideals.

Moreover, the kingdom's maritime connections forged links with Ireland that lasted centuries. These links provided economic lifelines, cultural inspiration, and military alliances. Dalriada's strong reliance on seaborne travel anticipated Scotland's later focus on controlling the seas for defense, commerce, and expansion. In many ways, Dalriada stood at the crossroads of Celtic Ireland and the emerging polities of northern Britain. Its rulers needed diplomatic skills as much as martial prowess to survive and adapt in a complex environment.

While Dalriada did not become a large empire, it endured long enough to pass on its Gaelic heritage, weaving it into the broader tapestry of Scottish identity. The seeds sown in Argyll would continue to grow, culminating in a kingdom that blended Pictish, Gaelic, and other influences. That blending process—marked by alliances, warfare, and religious development—will become even clearer as we turn to how Scotland's early kingdom took shape.

CHAPTER 6

THE FORMATION OF THE EARLY SCOTTISH KINGDOM

1. Introduction

By the 9th century, the mosaic of Pictish kingdoms and the Gaelic kingdom of Dalriada was changing. Repeated Viking raids had weakened coastal areas, Pictish leadership was in disarray, and Gaelic rulers were maneuvering for greater power. Out of these turbulent conditions arose the foundation of what we now call the early Scottish kingdom—a realm sometimes referred to as "Alba." Although centuries would pass before the modern idea of "Scotland" took solid shape, this period marks a turning point.

This chapter will explore how Gaelic and Pictish realms gradually merged. We will examine the roles of key figures, including Kenneth MacAlpin (Cináed mac Ailpín), as well as the broader political, religious, and cultural forces that encouraged unification. We will see that forming an early Scottish kingdom was neither sudden nor straightforward. Instead, it was a dynamic process influenced by Viking pressure, clan alliances, and the evolving ties between church and crown. By the end of this chapter, we will have a clearer view of how a unified Alba set the stage for the medieval Scottish monarchy.

---

2. The Context of Turbulence and Opportunity

In the decades leading up to the mid-9th century, many factors contributed to the decline of distinct Pictish dominance:

1. **Viking Raids:** Starting in the late 8th century, Viking fleets attacked monasteries and coastal forts, draining resources and morale. Pictish strongholds in the north and east bore the brunt of these assaults, weakening local rulers.
2. **Internal Power Struggles:** Pictish kingship was often contested among rival noble families. Without a stable royal dynasty, the

kingdom struggled to organize a united defense against external threats.
3. **Cultural Overlap with the Gaels:** Over generations, Pictish and Gaelic dynasties had intermarried, creating blurred lines of succession and alliances. Influential Gaelic families sometimes claimed Pictish titles or land through maternal inheritance, further intertwining the two worlds.

Meanwhile, Dalriada itself faced Viking aggression on its western coasts, yet certain Gaelic dynasties proved more resilient or fortunate in battle. Some Gaelic leaders, having weathered the storms, spotted an opportunity to extend their influence into Pictish territory. As the Picts looked for strong leadership to fend off Vikings, a Gaelic claimant with partial Pictish ancestry might appear as a unifying figure.

---

3. Kenneth MacAlpin and the Traditional Narrative

Kenneth MacAlpin (Cináed mac Ailpín), who died around 858 CE, is traditionally credited by later Scottish chroniclers with uniting the Picts and Gaels under one crown. The classic story suggests that in 843 CE, MacAlpin—then King of the Gaels in Dalriada—somehow took advantage of a leadership vacuum among the Picts, proclaiming himself ruler of both peoples. Some medieval legends even claim he invited Pictish nobles to a banquet and treacherously killed them, thus seizing power. While dramatic, these tales might be more folklore than fact.

Modern scholarship suggests MacAlpin's rise was more gradual and less treacherous. He likely had a legitimate claim to Pictish rulership through maternal lines, as Pictish succession rules often recognized descent through the mother. If MacAlpin's mother (or grandmother) belonged to a Pictish royal lineage, he could press a claim for the Pictish throne while already holding the kingship of Dalriada. In a time of Viking chaos, this dual claim may have garnered enough support among nobles who desired a stable, decisive monarch.

Whether through cunning, inheritance, or a mix of both, MacAlpin emerged as a central figure. After his coronation, he is said to have shifted his power base to the east, possibly indicating a strategic move to secure the richer lowlands and better defend against Vikings. Over the ensuing decades, MacAlpin and his successors fought to maintain this precarious union, forging the core of what chroniclers would later call the Kingdom of Alba.

---

4. The Process of Unification

Even if Kenneth MacAlpin's accession was a key moment, the actual process of unification took many years. Multiple Pictish provinces still retained local rulers or sub-kings, and some Gaels in the west continued to assert their independence. The new "King of the Picts and the Gaels" had to negotiate with these local elites, offering them positions at court, church patronage, or land grants to ensure loyalty. Resistance likely flared up in certain pockets, forcing the king to crush revolts or bargain for fealty.

Moreover, Viking incursions did not cease. Coastal areas and river estuaries, whether in Gaelic or former Pictish lands, remained vulnerable to sudden raids. Kings after MacAlpin had to unify their realm's defenses—organizing local militias, fortifying strategic points, and forging alliances with neighboring rulers, including some Vikings who might be open to treaties. In time, these efforts helped reinforce the idea of a single kingdom under one monarch, rather than a patchwork of separate tribal lands.

The church also played a unifying role. Christian monasteries in both Gaelic and Pictish areas recognized the authority of a single king who protected their lands and supported the building of churches. Bishops and abbots could act as mediators, traveling between Gaelic Argyll and eastern Pictland, encouraging cooperation. As Gaelic customs gradually merged with Pictish traditions, religious festivals and saints' cults offered shared points of cultural identity. This convergence of interests, both secular and sacred, laid a stronger foundation for the emerging kingdom.

---

5. Changes in Language and Culture

One of the most significant outcomes of unification was the gradual spread of Gaelic culture eastward. Over time, Gaelic became the dominant language in the royal court and among the nobility, supplanting the old Pictish tongue. The reasons for this shift were multi-layered. First, royal power now rested with a Gaelic-speaking dynasty. Courts and legal assemblies used Gaelic for official business. Second, monastic centers in Iona and other Gaelic strongholds continued to wield spiritual influence, promoting Gaelic literacy in religious contexts.

Pictish, already a language with uncertain classification (possibly a Brythonic Celtic tongue with unique features), lacked an extensive written tradition by the 9th and 10th centuries. As Gaelic scribes produced annals, genealogies, and saints' lives, they established Gaelic as the literate language of the new kingdom. Over the course of a few generations, Pictish speech likely survived only in remote pockets before fading away entirely—though it may have left some imprint on local dialects and place names.

Simultaneously, Gaelic art forms, such as intricate knotwork and illuminated manuscripts, found an audience in the eastern regions. Stone carving in the east began to exhibit Gaelic-inspired crosses alongside older Pictish symbolism, indicating a blend of traditions. In architecture, hillforts or Pictish strongholds might have been adapted to Gaelic tastes, with royal halls or chapels. Through these cultural fusions, the monarchy gradually fostered a new sense of identity—one that combined the heritage of both Picts and Gaels.

---

6. The Early Kings of Alba

Following Kenneth MacAlpin, a series of kings ruled the newly formed realm. Names like Donald I (Domnall mac Ailpín), Constantine I (Causantín mac Cináeda), and Áed mac Cináeda appear in the annals. They faced challenges that tested the young kingdom's resilience. Viking pressure continued, with Norse settlers establishing footholds in Orkney, Shetland, and the Hebrides, as well as raiding the mainland. Internal disputes over succession flared up periodically, reflecting the Gaelic tanistry system and lingering Pictish rivalries.

Despite such turmoil, the monarchy worked to assert central authority. Constantine I, who ruled from around 862 to 877 CE, reportedly strengthened alliances with local nobles and possibly expanded territory northward. But he also had to deal with persistent Viking assaults. He died in battle against the Norse, showcasing the constant military threat overshadowing the kingdom. Successors like Áed, Giric, and Eochaid each had short, conflict-ridden reigns.

Yet the idea of Alba as a single kingdom persisted. Even when a king lost his throne through defeat or political intrigue, the institution of kingship endured. The monarchy provided a unifying focus, a point of reference for secular authority and church support. Over time, later rulers like Constantine II (r. 900–943 CE) would consolidate the realm further, forging more stable governance. Under Constantine II, the term "Alba" appears more often in sources, indicating that the identity of a new kingdom—distinct from Dalriada or Pictland—was gaining traction.

---

7. Viking Threats and Shifting Alliances

Throughout the 9th and 10th centuries, Vikings remained a powerful force in northern Britain. Their presence in the Western Isles, Orkney, and Caithness carved out new Norse-ruled territories. These Norse earldoms sometimes allied with the kings of Alba to fight common enemies, such as rival Viking bands or Anglo-Saxon forces from southern regions. At other times, they launched raids into the heart of Alba, destabilizing local communities and challenging the king's authority.

In response, Alba's kings often negotiated truces or recognized certain Norse leaders' autonomy in exchange for peace. Marriages between Norse earls and Gaelic nobles could seal alliances. However, these relationships could be unpredictable, as changing circumstances prompted new conflicts. The monarchy in Alba had to remain flexible—at times forging pacts, at times rallying its warbands to repel attackers. The constant need for vigilance, mobilization, and diplomacy shaped the kingdom's administration. Leaders recognized the value of centralized command, better coordination, and the fortification of strategic sites.

A further complexity was the presence of Strathclyde to the southwest, a Brittonic kingdom that also contended with Viking pressure. Sometimes Alba formed alliances with Strathclyde, and eventually the southwestern kingdom came under the influence of Alba's rulers. Similarly, the northern English (or Northumbrian) realm might be an ally or foe, depending on the situation. Alba's kings had to juggle multiple fronts, forging short-term alliances that could shift rapidly.

---

8. The Role of the Church in Consolidation

The Church remained a critical ally for the emerging kingdom. Monastic networks and bishops offered spiritual legitimacy to the king, while the king protected church lands and sponsored new religious foundations. As Gaelic replaced Pictish in royal and ecclesiastical circles, monastic scribes continued the tradition of writing annals that documented important events. These records, in turn, reinforced the concept of a single Christian kingdom under divine guidance.

Iona, though still influential, faced Viking raids that led some monks to relocate. Over time, other monastic centers on the mainland gained prominence. For instance, Dunkeld and St. Andrews (originally associated with Pictish worship of St. Andrew) became significant religious hubs under royal patronage. By endorsing these sites, the king bridged Gaelic and Pictish Christian traditions. Pilgrimages, relics of saints, and feast days offered communal experiences that transcended local identities. People from different regions gathered for worship, forging a collective sense of "belonging" that subtly supported the monarchy's unifying goals.

Additionally, the Church helped in the development of laws that blended Gaelic customs with Christian moral principles. Monastic councils or synods could address matters of ecclesiastical discipline, inheritance, or disputes over land. Through these assemblies, the kingdom's nobility and clergy interacted regularly, working through conflicts under the overarching concept of unity in Christ. Over time, such gatherings contributed to a more cohesive governance structure, even if local lords maintained considerable autonomy in their own territories.

9. Administration and Governance

Establishing a functional administration across diverse territories was no easy task. Early Alba did not have a fully centralized bureaucracy. Instead, the king relied on a network of local lords, abbots, and appointed officials. These individuals managed day-to-day affairs, collected taxes or tributes in the form of cattle and crops, and raised levies in times of war. The monarchy's ability to enforce unity depended on personal relationships and oaths of loyalty rather than impersonal systems.

Nevertheless, certain innovations emerged. The concept of "mormaers" (regional rulers or earls) gained importance. These were powerful nobles entrusted with controlling large regions, often corresponding to older Pictish provinces or Gaelic districts. They acted as the king's representatives, presiding over local courts and mustering fighting men when needed. In return, they enjoyed privileges such as collecting local dues and gaining a share of any plunder or tribute. Over time, the mormaer system would evolve into the earldoms central to medieval Scottish governance.

Royal justice was another avenue for consolidation. When disputes between nobles escalated, the king or his appointed judges might intervene, using a combination of Gaelic law, church decrees, and local tradition to reach a settlement. The king's ability to settle disputes fairly—or at least effectively—bolstered his reputation, enhancing unity. While bribery, factional intrigue, and personal vendettas remained common, the concept of a higher royal authority took root slowly, curbing the worst excesses of clan-based feuds.

10. Daily Life in the New Kingdom

For the majority of people—farmers, artisans, and small-scale traders—the formation of a single Scottish kingdom might have felt distant at first. They continued to live in small villages or farmsteads, bound by local ties of kinship and tradition. Gaelic language spread eastward, but regional dialects persisted. In areas where Pictish was once spoken, remnants likely lingered in local place names or family traditions. Over generations, though, these communities came to identify themselves as part of a larger entity, especially when paying tribute or receiving royal protection from Viking raids.

Agriculture remained a mix of pastoralism and cereal cultivation. Cattle were still the primary measure of wealth, supplemented by sheep, pigs, and horses. Oats and barley thrived better than wheat in Scotland's climate, forming the basis of bread and ale. Fishing and hunting contributed to the diet, while coastal trade brought salt, dried fish, and imported goods from Ireland or beyond. Towns were not yet common; trade centers were small, often near monastic sites or strategic river crossings. As the kingdom stabilized, a few of these centers grew, laying early foundations for later burghs.

Religious festivals, saints' days, and local fairs offered periodic gatherings where news spread about royal decrees or conflicts with Vikings. Storytellers and poets performed, bridging the old Gaelic traditions of Dalriada with the evolving identity of Alba. Over time, a new sense of belonging took root, as people realized their king was not just a distant figure but someone who claimed authority over all Gaelic- and Pictish-speaking regions now united under "Alba."

---

11. Relations with the Wider World

As the kingdom of Alba matured, it became increasingly aware of developments outside its borders. Contacts with Ireland remained strong—cultural, ecclesiastical, and familial ties ensured a steady flow of ideas and people across the Irish Sea. Pilgrims might journey to Irish monastic sites, just as Irish monks visited Scotland's Christian communities. This exchange shaped theological debates, liturgical practices, and even the art of manuscript illumination.

To the south, the Anglo-Saxon kingdom of Wessex was on a path to unify England under a single crown, particularly after repelling Viking invasions. This would eventually create a powerful neighbor to Alba. At times, Alba's kings negotiated boundaries with Northumbria or recognized overlordship from English kings in exchange for peace. Diplomatic marriages also served as tools to maintain stability, though tensions persisted over contested lands like Lothian. Meanwhile, to the north, the Norse Earldom of Orkney remained a semi-independent stronghold, sometimes raiding or forming alliances with Alba's enemies.

Trade networks linking the North Sea and the Irish Sea expanded. Flemish, Scandinavian, and even Frankish merchants occasionally ventured to Alba's coastal trading spots. These merchants brought weapons, fine textiles, and continental coinage, exchanging them for Scottish wool, hides, and salted fish. Though not yet robust, this commerce laid groundwork for economic growth in future centuries, tying the kingdom to European currents.

---

12. Succession and Stability

A persistent challenge for early Alba was the Gaelic tanistry system, which allowed various male relatives in the royal family to claim the throne. While this provided flexibility—preventing the monarchy from getting stuck with an incapable heir—it also led to frequent succession disputes. Rival branches of the ruling family might gather support among regional nobles, church leaders, or even Viking allies. King Constantine II, for example, spent much of his reign securing loyalty from mormaers and putting down rebellions.

Nevertheless, a pattern of continuity did form. MacAlpin's dynasty held onto the throne for many generations, gradually building a tradition of legitimate kingship. Some rulers, like Constantine II, reigned long enough to implement consistent policies and form lasting alliances. Others died young, destabilizing the kingdom, but the institution endured. Over time, Alba's kings refined methods to manage succession, sometimes naming a chosen heir during their own reign to reduce confusion. This did not eliminate power struggles, but it did increase the odds of a smoother transition.

As the monarchy stabilized, it gained further prestige. Foreign leaders recognized Alba as a unified kingdom, dealing directly with its kings. Ecclesiastical authorities blessed these rulers, anointing them at ceremonial coronations that underscored divine sanction. Combined, these elements gave Alba's royal house a level of respect that neither Dalriada nor the Pictish kingdoms had enjoyed independently.

---

13. Evolution of Identity

Throughout the 10th century, a collective sense of "Alba" began to take root. Gaelic language and culture dominated royal courts, the church, and the nobility, absorbing and transforming Pictish heritage in the process. Later chroniclers, writing in Latin or Gaelic, portrayed MacAlpin's unification as a heroic act of nation-building. While these narratives often simplified the messy process of assimilation, they helped shape how medieval Scots remembered their past.

At the same time, local and regional identities did not vanish. The western Highlands retained strong Gaelic traditions, shaped by maritime links to Ireland. The eastern lowlands, with older Pictish influences, gradually adopted Gaelic speech, but unique customs lingered. Noble families traced mixed lineages, preserving old alliances. Ecclesiastical traditions in places like St. Andrews still recalled Pictish founders, while acknowledging Gaelic leadership.

Yet a broader identity was emerging: the realm of the Scots, or "Scotia," as Latin writers sometimes called it. By the 11th century, references to "Picts" largely disappear from records, replaced by the notion of a united Scottish people under Gaelic-speaking kings. This shift would pave the way for further changes as new influences—like Norman knights—arrived in the 12th century, but that story lies beyond our current scope. For now, Alba was forging its identity as a single kingdom whose culture was largely Gaelic, shaped by the union of two once-distinct groups.

14. Challenges in the 10th Century

Though Alba was forming as a kingdom, the 10th century was anything but peaceful. Viking activity continued, sometimes erupting into major conflicts. The city of York, under Viking control for parts of the century, became a focal point for power struggles in northern Britain. Alba's kings occasionally allied with or opposed Norse rulers in York, depending on what served their interests. Meanwhile, tension with the English kings of Wessex—later the kings of a unified England—fluctuated. Diplomatic marriages and short-lived treaties alternated with raids and punitive expeditions.

Internally, mormaers vied for autonomy, especially in the distant territories north of the Grampian Mountains. Some alliances broke down, leading to feuds that the king had to either suppress or carefully mediate. Church properties, though nominally protected, could become pawns in political maneuvers if local rulers seized monastic lands or demanded tribute. The monarchy's ability to handle these crises determined whether Alba held together or risked splintering back into smaller realms.

Nevertheless, enough structure existed to keep the kingdom intact. As each new king took the throne, he inherited not only the crown but also an emerging administrative network, a recognized set of religious institutions, and an expectation among nobles that Alba would endure. These foundations, fragile as they sometimes were, marked a clear step forward from the fragmented politics of Pictish times.

15. Long-Term Significance of Early Alba

Looking back, the formation of the early Scottish kingdom was a defining moment. It set the stage for:

1. **Cultural Fusion:** Gaelic language and customs merged with Pictish traditions, creating a new national identity.

2. **Unified Defense:** By combining resources, Alba stood a better chance against Vikings and other external threats, fostering a more stable environment for growth.
3. **Administrative Evolution:** The concept of a single ruler supported by mormaers laid the foundation for the earldoms and later feudal structures of medieval Scotland.
4. **Religious Cohesion:** A unified church under a royal patron meant Christian traditions could flourish, shaping law, learning, and art.
5. **Diplomatic Standing:** As a recognized kingdom, Alba could negotiate with neighbors on more equal terms, influencing northern British politics for centuries.

Though still a small and relatively poor kingdom by European standards, Alba possessed a resilience drawn from its Celtic roots, mountainous terrain, and strong local ties. As it expanded or contracted over the next century, its monarchy would become a focal point for Scottish unity, weathering new challenges from within and beyond its borders.

CHAPTER 7

THE VIKING INVASIONS AND INFLUENCE

1. Introduction

By the late 8th century, a new threat appeared on Scotland's horizons: the Vikings. These seafaring warriors from Scandinavia—mainly Norway and Denmark—brought swift raids and, eventually, settlements along Scottish coasts and islands. Over time, their influence transformed not only warfare but also trade, culture, and political structures in regions they reached. In particular, the far north and western isles of Scotland became strongholds of Norse power, reshaping local societies and challenging existing rulers like the Picts, Gaels, and later the kings of Alba.

This chapter explores the origins of Viking incursions, early raids on monasteries, the establishment of Norse earldoms, and the deeper cultural impact that followed. We will see how Viking settlers and native communities adapted to each other, at times fighting bitterly, at other times cooperating for mutual benefit. By the chapter's end, you will understand how the Viking Age affected Scotland's landscape, alliances, and economy, paving the way for new power dynamics across the region.

---

2. The First Raids on Scotland's Shores

The earliest recorded Viking attack on Scotland took place in the closing years of the 8th century. While details vary in different sources, the monastery on Iona (off the west coast) is often cited as a target of these Norse raiders. For local monks, these sudden assaults were terrifying and destructive. Monasteries stored valuable items—precious manuscripts, altars, and relics—that Vikings could easily seize. The remote island settings of many monastic sites, which once provided peaceful isolation for spiritual reflection, were now dangerously exposed to swift ships arriving from the sea.

Over the next decades, more raids hit the Hebrides, Orkney, Shetland, and coastal areas of mainland Scotland. Vikings would land, loot monasteries or settlements, capture slaves, and depart before local defenders could mount a strong response. Such tactics gave Vikings an early reputation for cruelty and unpredictability. Local rulers struggled to adapt to this new threat. Pictish and Gaelic leaders, used to land-based conflicts, suddenly faced a mobile enemy whose longships could appear with little warning and vanish just as quickly.

The impact of these raids was severe. Some monastic communities never fully recovered, while others adapted by fortifying their sites, hiding treasures, or relocating to more defensible locations. Political leaders in coastal regions realized that controlling the sea routes was now vital. Over time, this awareness nudged local powers to think about naval defenses and alliances with other groups facing Viking pressure. These early raids set the stage for a longer period in which Norse influence would expand into permanent settlement.

---

3. Viking Settlement in the Northern Isles

Among the regions most deeply affected by Viking expansion were the northern isles of Orkney and Shetland. Sparse in population and rich in coastal resources—like fish, farmland, and strategic harbors—these islands became a prime target for Norse settlement by the early 9th century. Archaeological evidence, including Norse-style longhouses, pagan burials, and runic inscriptions, shows the presence of a substantial Scandinavian-speaking population in these islands before long.

Local Pictish communities in Orkney and Shetland likely faced displacement or assimilation. While some might have fled to the mainland, others intermarried with Norse settlers. Over time, Scandinavian language, customs, and laws took root, gradually overshadowing the older Pictish culture. This shift was so profound that Orkney and Shetland remained culturally Norse for centuries, long after other parts of Scotland developed distinct Gaelic or "Scottish" identities.

Key to this Norse dominance was the establishment of a ruling elite—later known as the Earls of Orkney. These earls oversaw local governance, collected tribute, and built alliances with powerful Vikings across the North Sea. Their control helped secure Orkney as a base for further raids or expansions, not just in Scotland but also in Ireland and northern England. For Norse adventurers, the northern isles provided ideal stepping stones into the wider British Isles. Meanwhile, the local populace found itself integrated into a Scandinavian power structure that recognized the King of Norway as an overlord or distant figure of authority.

---

4. The Hebrides and Beyond: Norse Influence in the West

Viking incursions were not limited to the north. The Hebrides—an extensive chain of islands off Scotland's west coast—also attracted Norse attention. By the early 9th century, Vikings began establishing seasonal camps, then permanent settlements. The rocky shores, sheltered bays, and abundant fishing grounds made these islands valuable for both sustenance and trade. Over time, the region experienced a cultural transformation similar to that in Orkney and Shetland, albeit with strong Gaelic influences from nearby Dalriada.

Gaelic communities in the Hebrides often had to negotiate, intermarry, or ally with Norse settlers. While some conflicts erupted—leading to raids on monastic outposts—other relations were more cooperative. New hybrid societies emerged, blending Norse and Gaelic languages, art, and traditions. We see evidence of this fusion in place names (many Hebridean locations carry Norse-derived names) and in archaeological sites featuring a mix of Gaelic roundhouse styles and Scandinavian longhouse elements.

The strategic position of the Hebrides also shaped broader power struggles. Control over these islands allowed Norse chieftains to project power into mainland Scotland and Ireland. Conversely, Gaelic kings, such as those of Dalriada (and later Alba), recognized that losing the Hebrides to Norse rulers weakened their defensive posture. Hence, the Hebrides became a zone of constant negotiation, shifting alliances, and occasional warfare. By the 10th and 11th centuries, the region would be known to many

72

as the Kingdom of the Isles, reflecting a blend of Norse and Gaelic leadership.

5. Norse Society and Economy in Scotland

Viking settlers did not only conquer; they also farmed, traded, and built communities. Once secure in places like Orkney, Shetland, and parts of the Hebrides, they established permanent farms, raising cattle, sheep, and pigs. Fishing and sea-based commerce flourished. The Norse, skilled mariners, forged trade links across the North Atlantic, connecting Scotland with Scandinavia, Iceland, the Faroe Islands, and beyond. Goods such as dried fish, wool, hides, and locally crafted items could be exchanged for iron, luxury products, and even precious metals from continental Europe.

In coastal towns or seasonal markets, Norse merchants sold items like walrus ivory (sourced from Greenland or Arctic voyages), furs, and amber. Scottish communities that once saw Vikings only as raiders began to recognize the economic advantages that Norse trade could bring. Some local chieftains or Gaelic lords cooperated with Norse traders, offering protection or docking rights in return for a share of profits. A portion of the population might have disliked the presence of these foreign settlers, but many adapted, especially where commerce or marriage alliances brought mutual benefit.

We also see new forms of governance in Norse-held regions. The concept of the "thing"—an assembly of freemen—became a central institution for settling disputes and making local laws. This assembly-based tradition left marks on local law codes, place names, and social structures in areas under Norse control. While not all elements of Viking society were welcomed by native peoples—particularly the practice of taking slaves—certain political customs and legal traditions did find their way into Scotland's evolving medieval framework.

6. Religious Shifts: From Paganism to Christianity

Early Vikings arriving in Scotland were pagans, worshipping gods like Odin, Thor, and Freyr. Archaeological sites in Orkney and the Hebrides sometimes reveal burial mounds with grave goods, reflecting Norse pagan funeral customs. However, as Norse settlers stayed longer in these regions, interactions with Christian communities grew. In some cases, marriage to local Christian women likely encouraged conversions. Missionaries, monks, or church leaders also reached out, baptizing Norse chieftains in hopes of bringing stability and peace to troubled regions.

Over time, many Viking descendants became Christian, blending new faith with older traditions in subtle ways. Church building increased, with local stone chapels constructed in Norse-dominated areas. Bishops aligned with either the Scottish or Norwegian hierarchy oversaw these communities, depending on political alignments. By the 11th century, most Norse-Scottish communities were at least nominally Christian, although folk beliefs and stories about old gods lingered in local folklore.

This religious blending further integrated Viking settlers into the broader cultural landscape of Scotland. Crosses with Norse motifs and Gaelic inscriptions, for instance, show how art and worship merged. Monastic centers sometimes benefited from Norse patronage, as newly converted chieftains sought spiritual favor and legitimation of their rule. While conflicts between pagan Vikings and Christian Scots never vanished instantly, religion eventually served as a bridge, helping to unify populations that had once viewed each other with mistrust.

---

7. The Impact on Local Rulers: Picts, Gaels, and the Rise of Alba

For existing rulers in northern Britain, the Viking onslaught meant both danger and opportunity. The Pictish kingdoms bore the brunt of early raids, suffering damage to coastal settlements and monastic sites. Repeated Viking attacks contributed to political instability among the Picts, making it easier for Gaelic rulers—like Kenneth MacAlpin—to gain an upper hand. Over time, as we saw in previous chapters, the union of Picts and Gaels under the emerging kingdom of Alba formed partly in response to the shared need to resist Viking aggression.

In the west, the Gaels of Dalriada also faced Viking raids. Iona, their spiritual center, was sacked multiple times, prompting monks to relocate valuables or even move to Ireland. Nonetheless, certain Gaelic lords in the Hebrides learned to work with Vikings, forging alliances that ensured mutual profit through trade and raiding. Some Gaelic dynasties benefited from Viking pressure on Pictish territories, as it weakened potential rivals. The eventual merger of Pictish and Gaelic realms into Alba reflected the shifting balance of power in a Scotland where the Norse presence was now a permanent factor.

As the kingdom of Alba took shape in the 9th and 10th centuries, its rulers had to reckon with Viking-held territories in the north and west. Treaties, tribute, and occasional warfare defined relations with Norse earls in Orkney or Hebridean chieftains. The kings of Alba recognized that ignoring the Vikings was impossible; instead, they needed to control or at least neutralize Norse influence to maintain stability. Over the years, some Alba monarchs campaigned into Viking areas, while others sought marriages that tied Norse and Gaelic elites together.

---

8. Viking Influence on Place Names and Language

One of the clearest signs of Viking settlement and integration is the abundance of Norse-based place names across northern and western Scotland. In Shetland and Orkney, older Pictish names were largely replaced by Scandinavian terms for towns, islands, and natural features—examples include "Tingwall" (assembly field), "Kirkjuvágr" (Kirkwall), and "Hrossey" (Horse Island, now Mainland Orkney). In the Hebrides, many islands carry names derived from Old Norse, such as "Lewis" (from Ljóðhús) and "Uist" (possibly from Ívist).

This naming pattern indicates not just passing raids, but lasting occupation. Norse settlers named new farms, fields, bays, and hills in their own tongue, reflecting ownership and everyday use. Over time, Gaelic and Norse languages coexisted in many communities, forming a bilingual environment. Loanwords traveled in both directions. The local Gaelic dialect absorbed certain Norse terms, especially for maritime activities or new legal concepts. Meanwhile, Vikings living in Gaelic-speaking areas picked up local words related to farming or social organization.

Even after Norse political power waned in some regions, these place names survived as a cultural imprint. Today, they remain a visible reminder of Viking heritage in Scotland's geography. They also signal that the legacy of Norse settlement extends beyond conflict, encompassing shared life and blended traditions that shaped the evolution of Scotland's linguistic and cultural mosaic.

---

9. Norse Earldoms: Orkney's Ascendancy

By the 10th century, Orkney had emerged as a major Viking power center under a line of Norse earls. The most famous of these would later appear in the **Orkneyinga Saga**, a Norse saga recounting the deeds of the earls of Orkney. Although partially legendary, the saga preserves details about alliances, feuds, and Viking expeditions across the North Sea. It portrays Orkney's earls as ambitious rulers who sometimes recognized the King of Norway as their overlord but acted independently in local matters.

From Orkney, Vikings could raid or trade with the Scottish mainland, Ireland, the Hebrides, or England. Some earls also launched expeditions to Iceland and further. In times of strong leadership, Orkney's power overshadowed neighboring Norse territories, even dominating Shetland and parts of Caithness on the Scottish mainland. These earls might forge alliances with Gaelic lords or with the kings of Alba, seeking either to protect their holdings or expand them at the expense of weaker rivals.

However, Orkney's earls had to tread carefully. They faced internal rivalries among their own kin, while also balancing relations with Norway's monarchy and Scotland's growing kingdom. Sometimes, an earl married into Scottish royal lines, or a Scottish king recognized the earl's authority in exchange for tribute. This uneasy dance of politics ensured that Orkney remained a semi-independent hub of Norse culture well into the medieval period.

10. Viking Influence on Weaponry and Shipbuilding

The Viking Age also brought changes in military technology and seafaring. Norse longships, with their shallow drafts and wide sails, revolutionized naval capabilities in Scottish waters. Local rulers, seeing the Vikings' success at swift attacks, began to adapt their own vessels for speed and maneuverability. Over time, Gaelic and Pictish warbands started incorporating small galleys for coastal patrols. Although never matching the scale of the Norse fleets, these improvements helped local forces respond more effectively.

In terms of weaponry, Viking swords, axes, and spear designs influenced Scottish warfare. The broad axe, in particular, became an iconic Norse weapon that found its way into the arsenals of northern warriors. Armor and shield styles also saw gradual adoption. Some Gaelic or Pictish artisans began crafting hybrid designs that mixed Celtic decorative motifs with Norse shapes. Wealthy chieftains who wanted the best equipment sometimes imported blades forged in the Frankish realms, which Vikings traded widely.

These exchanges went both ways. Vikings in Scotland encountered Celtic styles of artistry, including elaborate knotwork. Some Norse smiths incorporated these patterns into metalwork, resulting in a distinctive blend often seen in jewelry or sword hilts. While conflict remained the norm, the cross-cultural sharing of technology and art quietly reshaped local craftsmanship and martial aesthetics, leaving archaeological finds that illustrate an interconnected world.

11. Societal and Cultural Interactions

Beyond the political sphere, everyday life in Viking-held territories reflected a complex mix of old and new. Settlers arriving with families sought permanent homes, and their children grew up in a world shaped by multiple influences. In some places, Gaelic and Norse communities lived side by side, each retaining distinct traditions but occasionally cooperating in tasks like fishing, seasonal harvests, or defense against outside threats. Over time, the boundaries between "native" and "Norse" blurred, especially through intermarriage.

This blending is evident in personal adornments. Brooches, pins, and amulets with combined Gaelic and Norse motifs appear in archaeological contexts. The same can be said of house styles: a settlement might feature a Gaelic roundhouse, a Norse longhouse, and transitional forms that borrow from both traditions. Shared feasting traditions also emerged, with references in later literature to gatherings that included Gaelic music and Norse sagas.

Meanwhile, the practice of slavery cut across cultural lines. Vikings were known to capture slaves on raids, including monks, peasants, or lower-ranking warriors. These enslaved individuals could be traded abroad or absorbed into local households. Native chieftains might also adopt Viking methods of capturing and ransoming enemies. Though grim, this reality added another dimension to the societies forming in Viking-influenced regions. Over time, some slaves gained freedom and integrated, further complicating the cultural tapestry.

---

12. Viking Raids on Deeper Mainland Territories

While many Viking activities focused on coastal or island targets, Norse expeditions did not stop at the shoreline. Some ventured deeper into mainland Scotland, following rivers like the Tay or the Clyde. They sought opportunities for plunder—monasteries, wealthy estates, and trade centers were prime targets. At times, Vikings established temporary camps inland, using them as staging points for raiding across multiple regions. Local rulers, if caught off guard, had little choice but to pay tribute or flee.

The kingdom of Alba, in its formative years, strove to contain these threats. Kings might gather local forces to ambush Viking groups in difficult terrain or set up defensive positions near river crossings. Some Gaelic lords learned to strike deals with Viking leaders, offering safe passage or small tributes in exchange for sparing certain areas. The success of these strategies varied. Records of repeated Viking onslaughts into areas like Dunkeld or Perthshire suggest that no single approach guaranteed safety.

Despite the chaos, some mainland communities discovered ways to benefit indirectly from Viking presence. Cities or towns that catered to Norse merchants could thrive, creating early "proto-burghs" where trade goods changed hands. A few Gaelic or Pictish warriors even joined Viking bands for a share of loot, forging cross-cultural alliances rooted in opportunism. These shifting loyalties show that the Viking Age in Scotland was not simply "us versus them," but a dynamic period of changing alliances, economic openings, and survival tactics.

13. Assimilation, Hybrid Identities, and the Decline of Raiding

By the 10th and 11th centuries, Viking raiding as a primary activity began to wane. Many Norse settlers transitioned from quick plundering to long-term governance, trade, and farming. Newly converted Viking leaders had fewer incentives to raid Christian sites, especially if they saw themselves as part of the local Christian community. Also, growing states in Norway, Denmark, and England demanded loyalty and resources from their subjects, reducing the number of freelance raiders looking for easy wealth.

In Scotland, Norse enclaves from Orkney to the Hebrides became more settled, forming stable societies that recognized either Norway's king or local earls as overlords. Gaelic-speaking populations within these enclaves also adjusted, adopting certain Norse customs while preserving older Celtic traditions. Over generations, a "Norse-Gael" identity emerged, particularly in the Hebrides, Isle of Man, and parts of western coastal Scotland. These Norse-Gaels spoke a form of Gaelic infused with Norse terms, practiced a Christian faith blended with older customs, and built maritime networks linking Ireland, Scotland, and Scandinavia.

The waning of Viking raids did not mean an end to conflict—far from it. Local feuds, dynastic struggles, and larger power plays continued. But the intense period of sudden, devastating assaults on monasteries and rural communities receded, replaced by more structured political competition.

Many historians see this shift as part of the larger European trend: a move from the "Viking Age" of roving warbands to more centralized medieval kingdoms and principalities.

---

14. Political Legacies and the Emergence of a New Map

By the late 11th century, the map of Scotland bore the stamp of Viking engagement. Orkney and Shetland remained under strong Norse influence, ruled by powerful earls who owed nominal allegiance to Norway. Parts of the northern mainland, like Caithness, also saw significant Norse settlement and governance. In the west, the Kingdom of the Isles, under Norse-Gael lords, straddled maritime routes between Ireland and Scotland. Alba's kings recognized these territories but often lacked direct control, leading to ongoing friction over boundaries, taxes, and loyalty.

Still, the kingdom of Alba grew stronger. As it consolidated, future kings would attempt to bring Norse-dominated regions under Scottish authority. Gradual expansion into areas like Moray and Ross eventually pressed up against Orkney's sphere of influence, igniting new rivalries. Over centuries, treaties, marriage alliances, and occasional wars would reshape the balance between Scottish monarchs and Norse earls. At the same time, shifting Norwegian priorities sometimes left the earls of Orkney to act with relative autonomy.

This complex patchwork of power highlights the Vikings' lasting political impact. They did not simply raid and vanish; they carved out domains, integrated with local cultures, and gave rise to new polities that outlived the initial wave of violence. Scotland's future kings inherited a land of multiple identities—Gaelic, Norse-Gael, older Pictish enclaves, and a growing sense of "Scottishness" in the kingdom of Alba. Navigating these identities required diplomatic skill as well as military strength.

---

15. Cultural and Genetic Heritage

Modern research, including place-name analysis and genetic studies, confirms that Viking-era settlement left an enduring legacy. Many individuals in the northern and western isles have ancestry tracing back to Norway and other Scandinavian regions. Language, folklore, and oral traditions in places like Shetland include remnants of Old Norse vocabulary, reflecting centuries of usage even after official ties to Norway waned. Local festivals, stories of trolls or sea spirits, and certain crafts—like knitting patterns or boat designs—hint at the continued cultural resonance of Viking heritage.

This blending did not produce a single homogenous identity. Instead, it created a mosaic, where Gaelic, Norse, and later Norman or Anglo influences overlapped. In Shetland, for instance, the old Norse law system called "Udal law" persisted well into later centuries, shaping property rights and inheritance differently than in mainland Scotland. Some Hebridean families bore Gaelic patronyms but boasted Norse ancestry or genealogical legends linking them to heroic Vikings. These complex lineages exemplify how deeply the Vikings influenced Scottish lineage and clan histories.

Even the Gaelic language itself absorbed Old Norse terms, particularly for maritime activities, local governance, and everyday objects that had no Celtic equivalent. Over time, these terms were fully "Gaelicized," though their origins remained. Thus, the Norse presence in Scotland is not just an episode of raiding but a key chapter in the country's cultural evolution.

CHAPTER 8

THE EMERGENCE OF THE KINGDOM OF ALBA

1. Introduction

In previous chapters, we observed how Vikings challenged Scotland's coastal areas, and how Pictish and Gaelic peoples united to form a fledgling realm often referred to by scholars as "Alba." By the late 9th century, Kenneth MacAlpin and his successors had begun forging a single kingship that blended Pictish and Gaelic power structures. Yet the kingdom's growth into a more cohesive state required several generations of political maneuvering, warfare, religious leadership, and cultural integration.

This chapter explores the development of Alba from the late 9th through the 10th and early 11th centuries—a period marked by shifting alliances, conflicts with Viking earls, battles with English rulers, and a strengthening internal administration. We will see how kings like Constantine II and Malcolm I expanded territories, enforced royal authority, and worked closely with the Church to bolster their legitimacy. By the end, Alba had taken shape as a kingdom recognized by its neighbors, laying the foundations for what would, in time, become medieval Scotland.

---

2. Consolidation Under MacAlpin's Descendants

Kenneth MacAlpin, often credited with uniting Picts and Gaels, died around 858 CE. His immediate successors—Donald I, Constantine I, and Áed—faced the daunting task of solidifying this new realm. Viking raids continued, with Orkney-based Norsemen probing eastern coasts and Hebridean Vikings harrying western shores. Internal disputes also flared. Pictish elites who had lost status under Gaelic leadership sometimes rebelled, while Gaelic nobles jockeyed for position in the young royal court.

Nonetheless, the monarchy persisted. Donald I (Domnall mac Ailpín) ruled briefly, with little recorded detail about his reign. Constantine I (Causantín mac Cináeda) then faced near-constant pressure from the Vikings. By the time Constantine I died in battle against Norse forces in 877 CE, it was clear that Viking aggression was a permanent reality. Despite setbacks, the idea of a unified kingship survived. The successive kings built on MacAlpin's legacy, learning to manage Viking threats through both military campaigns and tactical alliances.

Áed mac Cináeda's short reign ended in crisis, but his successor, Giric, attempted to expand control into Strathclyde, forging alliances with Brittonic leaders. Each ruler had to cope with local power structures still shaped by old Pictish provinces or Gaelic clans that expected recognition of their rights and traditions. Holding such a realm together required careful negotiation, intermarriage with regional dynasties, and grants of land or titles to secure loyalty.

---

3. Constantine II (r. 900–943 CE) and the Shaping of Alba

A pivotal figure in Alba's consolidation was Constantine II, who ruled for over 40 years. His lengthy reign allowed for a measure of stability that many earlier kings had lacked. Constantine II continued to face Viking threats, particularly from Norse-Gael rulers in the west and the Earl of Orkney in the north. Yet he also pursued alliances when convenient, minimizing open warfare.

During Constantine II's era, we see the term "Alba" used more frequently in sources, reflecting a distinct identity separate from Pictland or Dalriada. While Gaelic language dominated the court, older Pictish loyalties had not vanished. Constantine II had to balance these concerns, ensuring that leading families—Pictish, Gaelic, or mixed—felt included. He did this by arranging marriages, appointing nobles to key positions, and expanding the role of the Church as a unifying institution.

Relations with England were another concern. The Anglo-Saxon kingdom, under Edward the Elder and later Athelstan, was solidifying its control over much of southern Britain. These kings sometimes demanded tribute or cooperation from Alba's rulers to fend off Vikings. Constantine II participated in at least one major encounter, the Battle of Brunanburh (937 CE), where an allied force of Scots, Strathclyde Britons, and Norse-Gaels fought against King Athelstan of England. Although the allies lost the battle, it demonstrated Alba's ability to form coalitions and project power beyond its own borders.

By the time Constantine II retired to a monastic life in 943 CE—an unusual step for a king—he left behind a kingdom that had weathered major challenges. Alba was recognized as a political unit, its kings dealing as equals (or near equals) with English and Viking rulers. The stage was set for future monarchs to refine and strengthen royal authority within Alba itself.

4. Royal Administration and the Growth of Mormaerdoms

One key element in Alba's internal development was the rise of regional magnates known as mormaers. These officials, often drawn from powerful local families, governed large districts—roughly equivalent to later earldoms—like Moray, Fife, Atholl, or Angus. The mormaer owed allegiance to the king, collecting taxes or tribute, mustering local warriors, and upholding the king's justice. In return, they enjoyed considerable autonomy within their territories.

This system allowed Alba's rulers to manage distant provinces without a large, centralized bureaucracy—something that didn't yet exist. Because roads were few and the terrain challenging, direct royal oversight in every corner of the kingdom was not feasible. Instead, mormaers acted as the king's representatives, while also serving their own family interests. Not surprisingly, conflicts arose when a mormaer felt the king threatened local privileges. On the other hand, loyal mormaers provided crucial support against rebellious nobles or external foes.

Over time, these regional authorities became deeply woven into Alba's social fabric. Marriage alliances tied the royal family to leading mormaer dynasties, creating a network of interlinked genealogies. Church lands and appointments added another layer, as bishops or abbots sometimes belonged to noble lineages. Such ties produced a measure of unity, though tensions never disappeared entirely. Still, the overall effect was a more cohesive kingdom, where recognized authorities governed large swaths of territory under the crown's broad oversight.

5. Religious Foundations and Monastic Influence

Another stabilizing factor was the continued growth of Christian institutions. By the 10th century, the church in Alba had emerged from the turbulence of the Viking Age, reestablishing monasteries or founding new ones in safer inland locations. Monks and bishops played dual roles: they were spiritual leaders and also keepers of records, genealogies, and laws. Their writings shaped how people remembered Alba's early kings, often emphasizing divine support for the monarchy.

Kings like Constantine II and Malcolm I recognized the church's value as a unifying force. They granted land and privileges to monastic communities, who in return offered prayers for the royal family and provided moral justification for the king's rule. Religious ceremonies, such as coronations or the consecration of churches, became public events that showcased the alliance between crown and cross.

A notable example is the prominence of St. Andrews in Fife as a religious center. Originally associated with Pictish devotion to St. Andrew, it gradually became a focal point for national worship in Alba. As the monarchy supported St. Andrews with endowments, relics, and pilgrim traffic, the site grew in prestige. Bishops there, aligned with the king, could claim spiritual authority over large regions, further blending Pictish and Gaelic legacies into a shared Christian tradition.

6. Military Tactics and Defense

Though the kingdom sought unity, the reality of ongoing threats demanded robust military responses. Viking incursions into coastal areas did not vanish, and the earls of Orkney maintained ambitions on the mainland. Meanwhile, alliances with Strathclyde or Northumbria could turn sour.

Alba's kings needed a system to quickly gather forces, whether to repel invasions or to enforce royal authority over rebellious nobles.

The tradition of calling out local levies—men from each district—to form an army remained crucial. Mormaers were responsible for assembling and leading these troops, who were mostly infantry armed with spears, axes, or bows. Nobles and their personal retinues might possess higher-quality weapons or horses, but large-scale cavalry never became the mainstay of Scottish armies at this stage. River fords, mountain passes, and coastal headlands served as natural choke points. Defending these locations reduced the kingdom's vulnerability, especially against Viking raiders confined to waterways or ships.

To improve coastal defense, some kings supported the construction or reinforcement of fortresses along major river estuaries and sea inlets. Wooden palisades, earth ramparts, and stone walls protected strategic sites. While these fortifications could not stop a determined Viking fleet, they slowed attackers, giving defenders time to rally. Over time, Alba's leaders gained experience in maritime strategy, collaborating with local seafaring communities to scout or intercept enemy ships. Although the kingdom never matched the full naval prowess of the Vikings, it took steps to limit the damage from seaborne raids.

7. Relations with Strathclyde and the Britons

Strathclyde, a Brittonic kingdom centered around the Clyde valley, had long been an independent player in northern Britain. However, Viking raids and pressure from Anglo-Saxon territories weakened Strathclyde over the 9th and 10th centuries. Alba's kings sometimes allied with Strathclyde's rulers to face common threats, such as powerful Norse-Gael warlords or English kings pushing north. In other instances, Alba's expansionist aims clashed with Strathclyde's desire for autonomy.

Over time, ties between the two realms grew stronger, especially through royal marriages and shared campaigns. The Brittonic language of Strathclyde did not simply vanish, but Gaelic began to spread in the region through Alba's influence. By the early 11th century, Strathclyde was often treated as a sub-kingdom or client territory of Alba. Some references describe a "King of the Cumbrians," a subordinate ruler who recognized Alba's authority while maintaining local Brittonic traditions.

This process of absorption was not always peaceful. Rival claimants to Strathclyde's throne might seek support from Viking or English allies, leading to sporadic conflicts. Nonetheless, by the mid-11th century, Strathclyde was largely under Alba's sway, contributing to the kingdom's broader territorial consolidation. This development also helped shape Alba's cultural mix, incorporating Brittonic elements into the Gaelic-Pictish core.

8. Interaction with the English Kingdom

Meanwhile, England was coalescing under a unified monarchy, first under the House of Wessex and later under new dynasties. Relations between Alba and England oscillated between war and diplomacy. Kings of England, such as Edward the Elder or Athelstan, sometimes demanded submission or tribute from Alba's rulers to ensure the Scots wouldn't support Viking rebels. Conversely, Scottish kings looked for chances to assert independence or even expand south if English power faltered.

One of the most famous encounters was the previously mentioned Battle of Brunanburh in 937 CE, where King Athelstan defeated an alliance of Scots, Strathclyde Britons, and Norse-Gaels. The Anglo-Saxon poem celebrating the victory claimed it as a great triumph, underscoring the threat posed by such a coalition. Despite the defeat, Alba remained intact, suggesting that the English monarchy could not fully control the north. Indeed, subsequent English rulers had to negotiate or fight repeated conflicts near the borderline region, which was not yet the modern boundary.

Marriages between Scottish and English royal families became another tool of diplomacy. Princesses from England might marry into Alba's monarchy, or vice versa, hoping to secure peace. These unions sometimes produced alliances that lasted as long as the reigning kings lived, but they could unravel if a new king emerged with different priorities. Nevertheless, the mutual awareness of each other's power and shared concern about Viking threats kept Scotland and England in a complex relationship of rivalry, respect, and necessity.

9. The Changing Face of Gaelic Culture in Alba

As Alba expanded and absorbed diverse territories, Gaelic language and customs took hold as the primary culture of the royal court. This "Gaelicization" included everything from legal traditions to art and literature. Poetry, oral histories, and genealogical recitations—maintained by Gaelic filí (poets or bards)—reinforced the monarchy's legitimacy. The fusion of older Pictish influences persisted, but Gaelic forms dominated official expressions of power.

Yet Gaelic culture in Alba was not static. The presence of new influences—Viking, Brittonic, and Anglo-Saxon—left marks on dialect, personal names, and material arts. Some Gaelic noble families claimed partial Viking ancestry, showcasing their lineage's prestige or warrior tradition. Ecclesiastical art, such as illuminated manuscripts or carved stones, displayed motifs that combined Celtic spirals with Norse or Anglo-Saxon interlace patterns. Over time, these hybrid styles formed a distinctive visual language that appealed to elites eager to project a cosmopolitan identity.

Moreover, the church contributed to literacy in Latin, especially among clerics and some nobles. Latin documents recorded royal charters, land grants, and legal texts. The Gaelic oral tradition thrived alongside this Latin writing, meaning bilingual or trilingual skills were advantageous at court. This blend of languages and artistic styles prepared Alba for future centuries, when new waves of continental European influence would reshape Scottish society once again.

10. The Reign of Malcolm I and His Successors

Following Constantine II's retirement, a series of kings sought to strengthen the realm further. Malcolm I (Máel Coluim mac Domnaill), who ruled around 943–954 CE, expanded Alba's influence into parts of Strathclyde and possibly took advantage of power vacuums left by Viking battles in the west. He forged alliances with local rulers, continuing the approach of balancing warfare with diplomacy.

Subsequent monarchs, like Indulf (Idulb mac Causantín) and Duff (Dub mac Maíl Coluim), faced their own challenges, including renewed Viking raids or internal nobility strife. Some died in battle or were deposed by rival claimants. Yet the kingdom did not fracture; the idea of Alba as a single entity continued under each new king. This resilience demonstrates how the monarchy had become a stable institution—despite ongoing threats, the kingdom's structure outlived individual rulers.

By the time of Kenneth II and Constantine III, we see further evidence of consolidation. These kings attempted to codify laws, encourage the church's role in governance, and bring mormaers into a tighter royal orbit. Not all attempts succeeded, and revolts or assassinations occasionally disrupted progress. Even so, each reign that passed without a total collapse of authority reinforced the notion that Alba was here to stay—a realm recognized by its neighbors and bolstered by a shared Gaelic core.

11. The Church's Role in Royal Succession

One noteworthy development in the 10th century was the evolving role of the Church in succession politics. While Alba still practiced a form of tanistry—where multiple male relatives might claim the throne—religious leaders began insisting on more orderly or sanctified successions. Monastic chroniclers, who recorded events, favored kings who protected church lands and contributed to religious foundations. A monarch seen as pious or aligned with church reforms gained moral standing that could dissuade rivals.

Conversely, kings who threatened monastic property or disregarded clerical advice might be condemned in written annals. This moral weight did not always stop violent overthrows, but it shaped how future generations interpreted those events. A usurper lacking church support risked condemnation as ungodly. Over time, this interplay between monarchy and clergy pushed the kingdom toward a slightly more centralized approach to succession, though it would take centuries before primogeniture (inheritance by the firstborn son) fully replaced Gaelic tanistry.

Additionally, pilgrimages or religious assemblies offered opportunities for kings to showcase generosity and devotion. By funding churches and shrines, rulers signaled their commitment to a higher purpose, fostering loyalty among believers and clergy. These actions also provided a setting for negotiations, where the king might settle disputes among noble families under the watchful eyes of religious figures, further cementing the crown's role as an arbiter and protector.

---

12. Cultural Symbols of Alba's Growing Identity

As the kingdom matured, symbols of royal authority became more pronounced. Kings began to use formal seals on documents (when writing was involved), featuring Gaelic or Latin inscriptions that declared their power in "Alba." Stone monuments or crosses might commemorate notable victories or express gratitude for divine protection. These public markers helped shape collective memory, binding communities to the royal narrative of a united kingdom.

One such symbol was the "Stone of Destiny" (also known as the Stone of Scone), which legend claims was used in the coronation of Scottish kings. While its early history is shrouded in myth, by the 10th or 11th century, the stone had become an important emblem of rightful kingship in Alba. Ceremonies around it likely included Gaelic chants, prayers, and the presence of leading nobles. This ritual symbolism strengthened the monarchy's claim as heir to both Pictish and Dalriadan legacies, now unified in a single realm.

Artistic expressions also played a role. Carvings on high crosses or church panels depicted biblical scenes alongside Gaelic ornamentation, reinforcing a sense of shared Christian identity that transcended local differences. While only a fraction of these artifacts survive, they point to a cultural atmosphere where the monarchy, nobility, and the Church collectively fashioned a distinctive "Alban" style. Such art proclaimed unity and continuity at a time when warfare and political turnover were still common.

13. Influence of External Events

Throughout this period, Alba was not isolated. Developments elsewhere in Europe affected it. For example, the decline of strong Viking kings in Norway sometimes gave more freedom to the Earls of Orkney, intensifying their involvement in northern Scotland. Conversely, when a Norwegian king exerted firm control, Orkney earls had less latitude to raid or expand. Each shift impacted Alba's security or alliances in the north.

In England, the rise of kings like Edgar the Peaceful (r. 959–975 CE) and Æthelred the Unready (r. 978–1013, 1014–1016) introduced new pressures. A peaceful king might negotiate borders with Alba, while a weak king could invite chaos if Vikings used northern England as a launching pad for attacks on Scotland. Across the Irish Sea, Norse-Gael dynasties in Dublin influenced the Hebrides. Some Gaelic lords in western Scotland allied with these Norse-Gael rulers, complicating the Alba king's authority in the region.

Alba's rulers learned to respond swiftly, forging short-lived alliances or offering tribute where necessary. At times, they even intervened in foreign power struggles if it served their interests—supporting one Viking earl against another, or harboring an exiled English noble who might repay the favor later. This flexible diplomacy helped Alba survive and, in some instances, expand.

14. Toward the High Middle Ages: Duncan I and Macbeth

By the early 11th century, the monarchy in Alba was passing through a transitional phase that would lead it into the High Middle Ages. The reigns of Malcolm II (r. 1005–1034) and Duncan I (r. 1034–1040) introduced new alliances and conflicts, including extended clashes with northern earls and border tensions with England. Malcolm II famously achieved a victory at the Battle of Carham (1018), pushing the frontier of Alba south of the River Tweed. This victory helped secure Lothian as part of the kingdom, further expanding Gaelic influence into a region once dominated by Northumbrians.

Duncan I's reign was troubled by internal dissent. He also faced challenges from the north, where Moray's local rulers, possibly of mixed Gaelic and Norse descent, held significant power. One such figure, Macbeth, defeated Duncan and claimed the throne in 1040. Though later portrayed in Shakespeare's famous play as a villain, Macbeth likely had a legitimate claim under Gaelic succession rules and ruled until 1057. His reign, by most historical accounts, was stable enough to allow for public works and church patronage. This underscores the continued complexity of Alba's monarchy, where rival branches of the royal family competed for the crown in accordance with Gaelic traditions rather than purely dynastic lines.

Macbeth's fall at the hands of Malcolm III (Duncan's son) eventually set the stage for further changes, including increased Norman influence in the late 11th century. Though that belongs to future chapters, it highlights how the kingdom of Alba was never static. New claimants, external influences, and evolving internal structures kept the monarchy in flux. Yet the foundations of a recognizable "Scotland" were firmly in place by the mid-11th century: a kingdom that spanned from the northern Highlands to the Tweed, united under a Gaelic-speaking crown, tempered by Norse interactions, and guided by a growing church hierarchy.

CHAPTER 9

THE REIGN OF MACBETH AND THE IMPACT OF THE NORMANS

1. Introduction

By the mid-11th century, the Kingdom of Alba (early Scotland) was still taking shape after centuries of merging Gaelic and Pictish societies, dealing with Viking threats, and forging its royal institutions. In this environment rose Macbeth, a king whose historical reign (1040–1057 CE) later became famous in fiction. However, Macbeth's real life differed from the tragic character in Shakespeare's play. Instead of the story of a cruel usurper, the historical Macbeth ruled within a Gaelic framework of succession, faced his own challenges of legitimacy, and appears to have presided over a relatively stable period—at least by the standards of the time.

Following Macbeth, a new wave of transformation arrived in Scotland with the Norman influence. After the Norman Conquest of England in 1066, nobles, warriors, and churchmen from Norman and other continental backgrounds began settling in Scotland. The Scottish kings in the later 11th and 12th centuries welcomed these newcomers, aiming to strengthen the kingdom with new skills in warfare, administration, and culture. This chapter explores Macbeth's reign, the transition to Malcolm III and his successors, and how Norman ideas changed Scotland's feudal structures, landholding, castles, and society.

---

2. Macbeth's Path to the Throne

The Gaelic system of kingship (often called "tanistry") did not guarantee a neat father-to-son succession. Multiple branches of the royal family might vie for power, each claiming legitimate descent. Macbeth was part of this extended network. His exact lineage is somewhat uncertain, but he was connected to the ruling house of Alba through marriage and blood ties.

King Duncan I, who preceded Macbeth, was possibly the grandson of Malcolm II. Duncan became king around 1034. Unlike the older Gaelic tradition of rotating kingship among different branches of a royal kin group, Duncan tried to centralize power around his line. This approach may have alienated some nobles, including those from the north, such as Moray, where Macbeth had strong connections.

The conflict that led to Macbeth's rise began with growing discontent in the kingdom, especially in the north. In 1040, Macbeth defeated and killed Duncan near Elgin. Unlike Shakespeare's version, there is little evidence of a foul personal betrayal. Instead, it appears Macbeth had a real claim and that Duncan's rule had been troubled. Once Duncan fell, Macbeth took the throne, presumably with the backing of important nobles who accepted his legitimacy under Gaelic laws of succession.

---

3. Macbeth's Reign: Reality Versus Legend

From 1040 until 1057, Macbeth controlled a kingdom still dealing with Viking threats and local power struggles. Records about his reign are limited, but surviving sources suggest a few notable points:

1. **Relative Stability**:
   Despite being remembered in later stories as a tyrant, Macbeth seems to have ruled with a measure of acceptance. This is indicated by the length of his reign—17 years was not common for a supposedly hated usurper. If large parts of the nobility had opposed him, they likely would have acted sooner.
2. **Christian Piety**:
   Chronicles hint that Macbeth was a patron of the Church. One source suggests he made a pilgrimage to Rome around 1050, distributing alms to the poor. This act implies that he was recognized abroad as king and had the wealth and security to travel. While we cannot confirm every detail, such a pilgrimage indicates at least some level of stability.
3. **Local Power Balances**:
   Macbeth likely focused on keeping the northern provinces—such as Moray—loyal, while also defending against Viking activity. The earls of Orkney remained active in the north; and the western seas, populated by Norse-Gael communities, posed constant risks.

However, no major crisis during Macbeth's reign is recorded that would signal a total collapse of order.
4. **Clashes with the English**:
In the south, the border with Northumbria remained a zone of tension. During Macbeth's time, the English were under various rulers, including Edward the Confessor. Although some skirmishes or diplomatic engagements might have occurred, there is no record of a decisive English invasion that toppled Macbeth.

While Shakespeare's play revolves around guilt, witches, and regicide, the real Macbeth seems more like a Gaelic king operating within a fluid system of rulership, alliances, and conflict. He was neither uniquely brutal nor uniquely saintly. Instead, Macbeth's image became distorted in later centuries, especially after the lineage that replaced him—descendants of King Duncan—sought to justify their own claims by vilifying him.

---

4. The Fall of Macbeth and the Rise of Malcolm III

Macbeth's downfall began with the ambitions of Malcolm III (later known as Malcolm Canmore), son of Duncan I. Malcolm had taken refuge, possibly in England or elsewhere, after his father's death in 1040. Over time, he gathered support to challenge Macbeth.

A key turning point occurred in 1054 when Siward, the powerful Earl of Northumbria, led an invasion into southern Scotland, possibly on behalf of Malcolm. They achieved some success, though Macbeth was not deposed immediately. The final confrontation came in 1057 when Macbeth was killed at Lumphanan in Aberdeenshire. His death opened the path for Malcolm to claim the throne, though Macbeth's supporters briefly installed Macbeth's stepson, Lulach, who also soon fell.

With Macbeth gone, the line of Duncan I regained the crown. Malcolm III reigned from about 1058 to 1093, ushering in significant changes that would shape the future of Scotland. While Macbeth's reign ended in defeat, it did not vanish from memory. Gaelic tradition, as well as monastic chronicles, kept various accounts of Macbeth—some praising him, others condemning him. Over centuries, his story merged with legend, particularly after

Shakespeare's dramatized retelling. Yet historically, Macbeth stands as a Gaelic king who, for nearly two decades, managed the challenges of 11th-century Scotland until the forces of succession swept him aside.

5. Malcolm III's Early Challenges

When Malcolm III ascended the throne, the kingdom was still vulnerable on multiple fronts:

- **Viking Threat**:
  Though Viking raids were less intense than in earlier centuries, Norse earls in Orkney and Norse-Gael lords in the Hebrides remained influential. Maintaining peace with these northern and western neighbors required both military readiness and occasional alliances.
- **English Relations**:
  Malcolm had ties to Northumbria, partly through the help he received in unseating Macbeth. However, England itself was going through changes that soon became seismic with the Norman Conquest of 1066. For the first few years of Malcolm's reign, English kings (like Edward the Confessor) generally sought to keep a stable border, but that stability was short-lived.
- **Internal Unity**:
  Malcolm needed to secure loyalty among the Gaelic nobility, who had been divided between Duncan and Macbeth. Some clans in Moray might have resented the new king, especially after Macbeth's death. Balancing the demands of local lords and the need to strengthen royal authority was a constant struggle.

Despite these hurdles, Malcolm III managed to assert himself. He consolidated power by rewarding loyal followers and neutralizing potential rivals. Over time, he recognized the need for fresh alliances and stronger ties beyond Gaelic Scotland. This recognition laid the groundwork for welcoming external influences—most notably, Norman and Anglo-Saxon refugees fleeing England after 1066.

6. The Norman Conquest of England (1066) and Its Ripple Effects

When William, Duke of Normandy, defeated King Harold Godwinson at the Battle of Hastings in 1066, England fell under Norman rule. This dramatic shift sent shockwaves throughout the British Isles. Many Anglo-Saxon nobles and warriors who lost their lands in England fled north, seeking protection and new opportunities. Malcolm III saw a chance to strengthen his kingdom by offering refuge to these skilled individuals, who brought administrative knowledge, military experience, and cultural ties to continental Europe.

Among the notable exiles was Edgar Ætheling, a claimant to the English throne. Edgar, along with his sisters Margaret and Christina, found safety at the Scottish court. Margaret's arrival would prove especially significant. She married Malcolm III, becoming Queen Margaret of Scotland. She and her Saxon entourage introduced new customs at court, influenced religious practices, and helped shape the kingdom's broader orientation toward European norms.

At the same time, William the Conqueror, now King William I of England, viewed Scotland's harboring of English rebels with suspicion. Tensions rose along the Anglo-Scottish border, leading to periodic confrontations. Malcolm launched raids into northern England, partly to test William's resolve and partly to protect his position as patron of Saxon exiles. William, in turn, led campaigns into southern Scotland, pushing Malcolm to submit or negotiate. The dynamic between England and Scotland grew more complex as Norman power solidified in the south.

---

7. Marriage of Malcolm III and Margaret: Cultural and Religious Influence

Margaret, later known as St. Margaret of Scotland, was a devout Christian of Anglo-Saxon royal blood. Her marriage to Malcolm III likely took place around 1070, marking a defining moment in Scottish history. She brought with her a refined sense of courtly behavior, influenced by the old English royal court and possibly some Norman manners. Over time, Margaret championed religious reforms, aligning the Scottish Church closer to Roman practices.

Some notable changes or influences attributed to Margaret include:

1. **Religious Observances**:
   Margaret promoted proper observance of Lent, encouraged the usage of Latin in church services, and introduced stricter fasting rules. She also engaged in charitable works, including feeding the poor and founding hostels for travelers.
2. **Literacy and Learning**:
   With Margaret's arrival, more English clerics and possibly Norman-educated churchmen joined Scottish religious communities. Latin-based literacy, scriptoria (writing rooms in monasteries), and the copying of religious texts received fresh support.
3. **Royal Court Etiquette**:
   Contemporary accounts suggest Margaret urged Malcolm to adopt a more refined court life—introducing table manners, ceremonial feasts, and new clothing styles. Although Gaelic traditions remained strong, the blend of Saxon and Gaelic customs created a more international atmosphere at court.
4. **Church Reforms**:
   Margaret convened synods (church councils) to discuss ecclesiastical discipline, sacramental practice, and the relationship between clerics and the Roman Church. While some Gaelic clergy resisted these changes, over time, Margaret's influence helped push the Scottish Church away from certain Celtic practices toward the standards recognized in England and on the Continent.

Margaret's personal piety and charitable reputation won her admiration. Long after her death in 1093, the Church canonized her for her devotion. She became a symbol of Christian virtue in Scotland, and her marriage to Malcolm III represented the kingdom's gradual pivot toward broader European engagement.

8. Norman Knights and Feudal Changes in Scotland

Even before Margaret's arrival, Malcolm III had shown interest in recruiting foreign knights, especially Normans. With the turmoil in England, many disinherited Norman or Anglo-Norman nobles were looking for land and status. Scotland offered opportunities if they pledged loyalty to the Scottish king. Over time, these newcomers brought the feudal ethos of Normandy—based on hierarchy, knighthood, and castle-building—into Scotland.

Examples of Norman families who gained prominence in Scotland include the Bruces, the Stewarts (originally from Brittany but associated with the Norman world), and the de Morvilles. These families received grants of land in strategic regions, such as the Lothians or along contested borders. In return, they owed military service and loyalty. This arrangement mirrored the feudal pattern taking shape in England after 1066, where the king granted fiefs to vassals in exchange for knights.

With these new lords came motte-and-bailey castles—earthwork-and-timber fortifications that were quicker to build than the traditional ring-forts or hillforts of Gaelic tradition. Over time, some castles were upgraded to stone keeps, marking a shift in how territory was defended and controlled. The presence of feudal obligations started blending with older Gaelic customs, where landholding was traditionally communal or clan-based. This gradual shift laid the groundwork for a more stratified social order, setting a pattern that would deepen in subsequent reigns.

---

9. The Reigns of Malcolm III's Sons and the Growth of Norman Influence

Malcolm III and Margaret had several children, many of whom became Scottish kings:

- **Duncan II** (briefly reigned in 1094),
- **Edgar** (ruled 1097–1107),
- **Alexander I** (1107–1124),

- **David I** (1124–1153).

These monarchs, known as the "Margaretsons," continued to integrate Norman and Anglo-Saxon influences into the kingdom. For instance, King Edgar maintained amicable relations with England, consolidating the link between the Scottish and English royal houses. Alexander I focused on church reforms and further castle-building.

The most transformative of Malcolm III's sons was **David I**, who reigned from 1124 to 1153. David I had spent part of his youth at the English court, under his brother-in-law King Henry I. There, David absorbed Norman governance methods, feudal law, and the importance of monasteries as both spiritual and economic engines. When he became king of Scots, David applied these lessons vigorously. He granted large tracts of land to Norman knights and monastic orders, encouraging them to found new abbeys and priories. Cistercian monasteries, such as those at Melrose and Dundrennan, appeared, promoting advanced agricultural practices and fostering literacy through scriptoria.

Under David I, a structured feudal system began to emerge, at least in the Lowlands. Titles such as "earl" replaced the older Gaelic "mormaer" in some areas, while sheriffdoms were introduced to administer royal justice. Royal burghs—towns with special trading rights—sprang up, further linking Scotland to European commerce. Though Gaelic culture remained dominant in the Highlands, the Lowlands took on a more Normanized character, bridging Scotland with the political and cultural currents of northern Europe.

---

10. Challenges and Resistance to Normanization

Not everyone welcomed these changes. Gaelic aristocrats in the north and west saw the rise of Norman lords as a threat to their traditional rights. Some clans viewed castle-building as an attempt to impose foreign control. In regions like Moray or Argyll, local rulers occasionally rebelled against the centralizing push. These uprisings, however, struggled against the coordinated power of feudal knights and the king's new administrative tools.

The Church reforms promoted by Margaret and her sons also met opposition in certain Gaelic monasteries accustomed to Celtic practices. While the Roman standard eventually prevailed, pockets of old traditions lingered. Tensions sometimes flared between Gaelic-speaking clergy and bishops who championed a more continental approach.

Moreover, the Highland-Lowland divide, which would become a recurring theme in Scottish history, began to take clearer shape. The Lowlands, closer to the English border and home to royal centers like Edinburgh, embraced Norman feudalism more rapidly. The Highlands and islands, distant from these developments, maintained older clan structures and Gaelic language. Over centuries, this divide would influence conflicts, cultural identities, and political allegiances in Scotland.

---

11. Securing Borders and Relations with England

As Norman influence grew in Scotland, the line between Scottish and English affairs blurred. Many Norman families held lands in both kingdoms, so their loyalty could be split. English kings, from William Rufus (r. 1087–1100) to Henry I (r. 1100–1135) and beyond, sometimes demanded homage from Scottish kings for territories in northern England. In exchange, Scottish rulers expected recognition of their independence north of the border.

When David I inherited the throne, he pushed to secure not only southern Scotland but also claims in northern England. He controlled the earldom of Huntingdon by marriage, giving him a seat among English nobility. This dual role complicated Anglo-Scottish politics: David was both a vassal in England and a sovereign king in Scotland. Eventually, disputes over territories like Northumberland led to battles, but David I's willingness to adopt Norman styles of rule helped him negotiate power in both realms.

Even after David's death, conflicts over the border flared. Successors like Malcolm IV and William the Lion struggled with English kings who wanted to reimpose control. The concept of a well-defined national boundary was still forming, and repeated invasions or treaties shifted the line back and forth. Still, the presence of castles, Norman knights, and a more centralized administration gave Scottish monarchs tools to hold their own.

12. Social and Economic Changes Under Norman Influence

The arrival of Norman knights and monastic orders also reshaped everyday life:

1. **Agricultural Innovations**:
   Monastic estates introduced new farming methods, such as improved plows and crop rotation. Cistercian houses, in particular, were adept at land management, clearing forests and draining marshes for cultivation. These changes boosted productivity in the Lowlands.
2. **Trade and Towns**:
   Norman feudal lords supported the growth of burghs—settlements with special rights to hold markets, collect tolls, and practice crafts. Towns like Berwick, Roxburgh, and later Aberdeen expanded, attracting merchants from Flanders, Germany, and elsewhere. This commercial activity spurred the rise of a merchant class, laying an early foundation for urban life in Scotland.
3. **Legal Structures**:
   Norman feudal law introduced written charters documenting land grants, privileges, and obligations. This reliance on charters promoted literacy and record-keeping among the elite. The concept of the "royal court" grew, with the king or his representatives hearing disputes. Although Gaelic customary law did not vanish, it had to adapt to the new, more formal environment in the Lowlands.
4. **Cultural Exchange**:
   Norman families and their retinues brought French language and chivalric ideals, influencing Scottish courtly culture. Over time, the Scots language emerged from an Old Northumbrian (Anglian) base, absorbing French vocabulary and Gaelic influences, especially in the Lowlands. Poetry, music, and art gained new elements reflecting a pan-European style.

Despite these transformations, much of the population—especially in rural areas—continued living in small farming communities. The interplay between old Gaelic ways and the new Norman-driven changes was not uniform, often leading to a patchwork of practices across the kingdom.

13. The Legacy of Macbeth and the Normans

When we look back at the era spanning Macbeth's reign to the strong Normanization under David I and his successors, we see a kingdom in transition. Macbeth stands at the end of the mostly Gaelic-led kingship, where succession still followed older Celtic patterns and power rested on clan-based allegiances. His defeat by Malcolm III opened the path for a royal house increasingly oriented toward Anglo-Saxon and Norman customs.

Over the following century, the Norman Conquest of England spilled into Scotland, bringing fresh blood, feudalism, castles, and ties to continental Europe. This surge of outsiders—some fleeing the Normans, others actively seeking land and privilege—ultimately knitted Scotland into the broader medieval world. It produced new social hierarchies, a stronger monarchy, and the seeds of a cultural divide between the Gaelic-speaking Highlands and the increasingly feudalized Lowlands.

But one should not overlook the threads of continuity. Gaelic language, clan traditions, and local customs remained robust, especially beyond the Lowland heartlands. The monarchy itself, despite adopting Norman practices, retained elements of Gaelic identity for centuries. The result was not a simple replacement of Gaelic society with Norman institutions, but a layered blending of influences—a pattern that would characterize Scotland's growth well into the medieval period.

14. Transition to Future Developments

By the early 12th century, the changes sparked by Macbeth's fall and the Norman influence were clear: the Scottish royal court had become more international, the Church more in line with continental standards, and the feudal system was taking root. These shifts set the stage for further consolidation under David I, who extended royal authority more uniformly.

Yet with growth came new tensions. The next major era of Scottish history would see the kingdom tested by power struggles, both internal and external. Rival dynasties within Scotland, as well as powerful English monarchs, would challenge the independence of the kingdom. Eventually, these tensions led to the dramatic conflicts known as the Wars of Independence—clashes that would redefine the nature of Scottish identity and kingship.

In the next chapter, we turn to **Scotland's Wars of Independence**. That period, beginning in the late 13th century, saw famous figures like William Wallace and Robert the Bruce resist English domination. They drew upon the structures, alliances, and cultural identities formed in these earlier centuries—a reminder that Macbeth's era and the Norman wave shaped Scotland's later ability to unite under a shared cause.

CHAPTER 10

SCOTLAND'S WARS OF INDEPENDENCE

1. Introduction

By the late 13th century, Scotland had evolved from a patchwork of Gaelic and Pictish territories into a kingdom influenced by Norman feudalism, with established ties to the wider medieval world. The royal dynasty traced back to David I and Malcolm III, blending Gaelic heritage with continental customs. This development, however, did not shield Scotland from the ambitions of powerful English kings. When a succession crisis struck Scotland in 1290, England's Edward I saw a chance to assert overlordship, sparking decades of conflict known collectively as the Wars of Independence.

These wars were not a single, continuous struggle but a series of interconnected campaigns, uprisings, treaties, and power plays. Key figures emerged—like William Wallace and Robert the Bruce—whose reputations still echo in Scottish memory. They fought to maintain Scotland's status as an independent kingdom, resisting English efforts to control the throne, land, and governance. In this chapter, we will trace the roots of the crisis, the main events and battles, and the eventual outcomes that shaped Scotland's identity for centuries to come.

---

2. Background: The Death of Alexander III and the Maid of Norway

A period of stability under King Alexander III (1249–1286) had left Scotland with a clear monarchy and some prosperity. However, tragedy struck in 1286 when Alexander III died unexpectedly after a nighttime accident on a coastal path. His surviving heir was his young granddaughter, Margaret, known as the Maid of Norway—so called because she lived at the Norwegian royal court. This precarious situation set alarm bells ringing among Scottish nobles, who worried about a child queen's ability to rule from abroad.

In 1290, plans were made to bring Margaret to Scotland for her coronation, but she died en route in the Orkney Islands. Her death threw Scotland's succession into chaos. Multiple claimants emerged, each with different genealogical ties to earlier Scottish kings. The nobility, anxious to avoid a civil war, agreed to let Edward I of England arbitrate—believing him to be a neutral figure. Unfortunately, Edward I used this role to demand recognition of his authority over Scotland.

3. The Great Cause and the Rise of John Balliol

The process to decide Scotland's new monarch became known as the "Great Cause." Thirteen claimants put forward their rights, but only two were truly serious contenders: John Balliol and Robert Bruce (the grandfather of the later King Robert the Bruce). Both had plausible descent from David I's lineage. Edward I reviewed legal arguments, drawing out the proceedings while cementing his position as feudal overlord.

In 1292, Edward chose John Balliol to be King of Scots, likely because he believed Balliol would be pliable. John was crowned at Scone, but his kingship was overshadowed by Edward's overlordship demands. Edward required Balliol to do homage and hear legal appeals in English courts—acts that undermined Scotland's sovereignty. Many Scottish nobles felt humiliated and rebellious. Balliol himself resented the interference but lacked a strong power base to resist effectively.

From the start, King John Balliol faced the impossible task of balancing Edward I's demands with his own people's desire for independence. When Balliol tried to form alliances with France—England's enemy—Edward I invaded Scotland in 1296, capturing key towns like Berwick and forcing Balliol to abdicate. Edward then stripped Scotland of its regalia and attempted to govern directly, placing English officials in charge. This heavy-handed rule set the stage for open resistance.

4. The Rise of William Wallace

Edward's occupation galvanized Scottish defiance. Many nobles were cautious, having sworn oaths to Edward or hoping to recover their lands through negotiation. But the common people and lesser knights found a leader in William Wallace, a minor noble from the area near Elderslie (Renfrewshire). Wallace's background is partly shrouded in legend, but early acts of resistance—like attacking English officials—made him a folk hero.

By 1297, Wallace was leading a growing rebellion. Joined by Andrew Moray (who led resistance in the north), Wallace challenged English garrisons across central Scotland. Their most dramatic success came at the **Battle of Stirling Bridge** (September 1297). Outnumbered Scots ambushed an English army as it crossed a narrow bridge over the River Forth. English knights and infantry, funneled into a tight crossing, were unable to deploy effectively. The Scottish forces cut them down, winning a staggering victory that shocked Edward's regime.

With Stirling Bridge, Wallace and Moray temporarily expelled many English troops, and Wallace was declared "Guardian of Scotland" on behalf of the exiled King John Balliol. Tragically, Andrew Moray died from wounds received in the battle. Wallace carried on, but the unity of Scottish nobles was far from complete. Still, for a brief moment, Wallace personified Scotland's hope for freedom from English rule.

---

5. The Battle of Falkirk and Wallace's Downfall

Edward I, furious at the defeat at Stirling Bridge, led a substantial army north in 1298. Wallace faced him at the **Battle of Falkirk** (July 1298). The Scots formed defensive schiltrons—tight circles or squares of infantry bristling with spears—but English longbowmen wreaked havoc on these formations. Knights on horseback then smashed through the weakened lines. The Scots were decisively beaten, and Wallace fled the field.

Though Wallace survived, his defeat eroded his political standing among nobles, many of whom had not fully supported him. He resigned the guardianship, and the struggle continued under other leaders. Wallace's activities over the next few years remain shadowy; he possibly pursued guerrilla warfare, traveled abroad to seek support from European rulers, or took part in smaller raids. Edward I put a massive bounty on Wallace's head, determined to crush any symbol of Scottish defiance.

In August 1305, Wallace was betrayed and captured near Glasgow. Transported to London, he was tried for treason, even though he had never sworn loyalty to Edward. The trial was a formality, and Wallace was executed in a brutal manner—hanged, drawn, and quartered. His body parts were displayed in several towns, a grim warning to others. Instead, Wallace's martyrdom only deepened Scottish resentment, ensuring his memory would inspire future generations.

---

6. Robert the Bruce's Path to Kingship

After Wallace's capture, leadership of the resistance fell largely to Scottish nobles jockeying for position. Key among them was **Robert the Bruce**, grandson of one of the Great Cause claimants. Bruce had a complex history, sometimes siding with Edward I, at other times leaning toward Scottish independence. This shifting loyalty reflected the uneasy choices faced by nobles who held lands in both Scotland and England.

Two major figures emerged: Robert the Bruce and John Comyn ("the Red Comyn"), both with royal blood. They disagreed about the best route to restore Scottish sovereignty—some favored restoring John Balliol, others sought a new king. In 1306, Bruce and Comyn met in a church at Dumfries, supposedly to negotiate an alliance. Their meeting turned violent, and Bruce stabbed Comyn, who died soon after. Killing a rival before an altar was considered sacrilege, forcing Bruce to act quickly.

Within weeks, Robert the Bruce raced to Scone, where he was crowned King of Scots in March 1306. His coronation lacked full ceremonial regalia, as Edward I had seized Scotland's royal treasures earlier. Nevertheless, this bold move set the stage for a renewed campaign of independence, now under Bruce's claim to the throne. Edward I responded harshly, capturing Bruce's family members and allies, executing some, and forcing Bruce into hiding.

7. The Guerrilla Phase and Bruce's Fight for Survival

Bruce's initial attempts to defend his crown were disastrous. He suffered defeat at Methven in 1306, then faced further setbacks in the north. Some accounts say he sought refuge in remote areas—perhaps on Rathlin Island or in the western isles—where he regrouped with a small band of loyal supporters. During this time, many considered Bruce's cause lost. Yet he refused to surrender.

Over the winter of 1306-1307, Edward I fell ill and died, leaving the English throne to his less formidable son, Edward II. With the "Hammer of the Scots" gone, Bruce found some breathing room. He returned to the mainland, shifting to guerrilla tactics—swift raids, ambushes, and surprise attacks on English garrisons. One by one, he defeated rival Scottish nobles who still opposed him and reclaimed key castles.

Bruce's resilience earned admiration. He showed mercy to some former enemies and forged new alliances through marriage or land grants. Slowly, the tide turned. By 1309, he held a parliament at St. Andrews, securing wider recognition as king. Gradually, Bruce's forces reclaimed territory, capturing or destroying English-held castles and reaffirming Scotland's independence in practice, though England had not recognized it legally.

8. The Battle of Bannockburn (1314)

The defining moment of Bruce's campaign came at **Bannockburn**, near Stirling Castle, on June 23-24, 1314. Edward II marched a large army north to relieve the English garrison at Stirling, which had agreed to surrender if not reinforced by Midsummer's Day. Bruce's smaller force took position near the Bannock Burn (stream), using the terrain—wooded areas, marshy ground—to offset English numbers.

On the first day, Scottish spearmen repelled English cavalry in a series of skirmishes. The next morning, the main battle commenced. Edward II's knights, massed in a confined space, struggled to break Bruce's well-prepared schiltrons. Panic spread among the English ranks as the Scottish defenders held firm. A sudden charge by Scottish forces, combined with the specter of local camp followers appearing over the horizon, caused the English to retreat in disarray. Edward II barely escaped with his life.

Bannockburn was a stunning Scottish victory. It did not end the war outright but shattered the myth of English invincibility. Bruce's prestige soared, and many of the remaining nobles who had been on the fence now rallied to him. Over the following years, Bruce consolidated his rule, recapturing more fortresses and conducting raids into northern England. Bannockburn became the symbol of Scottish courage and a cornerstone of national pride for centuries to come.

---

9. The Declaration of Arbroath (1320)

While Bruce had de facto control of most of Scotland after Bannockburn, formal recognition of Scottish independence remained uncertain. The Pope and other European powers needed clarity on who held legitimate authority. In 1320, Scottish nobles and church leaders sent a letter to Pope John XXII, known as the **Declaration of Arbroath**.

This document, written in Latin, is famous for its stirring defense of Scottish liberty. It asserts that Scotland had always been free and that the people had the right to choose their king. If Robert the Bruce failed them, they claimed they would select another. This bold statement challenged the feudal notion that kings ruled by divine appointment alone. Instead, it suggested a form of contractual relationship between ruler and ruled, at least in rhetorical terms.

The Declaration of Arbroath appealed to the Papacy to acknowledge Bruce's legitimacy and to urge England to recognize Scottish independence. While the Pope did not immediately force Edward II to surrender his claims, the letter made Scotland's case on the European stage. Over time, the Papacy grew more sympathetic to Bruce's cause, especially as Edward II's reign descended into domestic strife in England.

10. The Treaty of Edinburgh-Northampton (1328) and Aftermath

By the late 1320s, England was in turmoil. Edward II lost support among powerful English nobles and was eventually deposed by his wife, Queen Isabella, and her ally Roger Mortimer. His teenage son, Edward III, became king, but his government was controlled by Isabella and Mortimer. They needed peace on the northern border, particularly since they faced internal challenges at home.

In 1328, representatives of Scotland and England signed the **Treaty of Edinburgh-Northampton**, in which England recognized Scotland's independence and Robert the Bruce as its rightful king. Bruce, in turn, agreed to pay a monetary settlement and arranged a marriage between his son David and Edward III's sister Joan. This treaty was a landmark event, though it was not universally popular among English nobles. Some felt it was a humiliating concession.

Sadly, Robert the Bruce died the following year (1329). He left a young son, David II, as heir to the throne. Though the treaty was a diplomatic success, it did not guarantee lasting peace. A second phase of the Wars of Independence would erupt under David II's reign when Edward III, having taken full control of England, revived claims of overlordship. Yet the first phase of the wars ended with Scotland widely recognized as a separate kingdom, thanks to Bruce's efforts and the unified stand of the Scottish nobles.

11. Social and Economic Impact of the Wars

The Wars of Independence disrupted everyday life in Scotland. Raiding devastated border regions, farmland was frequently burned, and merchants faced difficult conditions for trade. Yet the conflicts also spurred changes:

1. **Rise of a National Consciousness**:
   The sense of fighting for a collective "Scottish" cause, represented

by figures like Wallace and Bruce, laid foundations for a stronger national identity. Clan rivalries did not vanish, but the unity displayed at battles like Bannockburn suggested that Scots could stand together against a common foe.

2. **Shift in Alliances and Nobility**:
Nobles who supported England risked losing lands. After Bannockburn, Bruce redistributed estates to loyal followers, altering the map of landownership. This gave rise to families who owed their status to Bruce's patronage.

3. **Church Support**:
Many church leaders backed the independence cause, seeing an English takeover as a threat to Scotland's ecclesiastical independence. Monasteries sometimes offered safe haven to rebels, and bishops helped negotiate truces. The church's endorsement of Bruce bolstered his legitimacy.

4. **Trade Relations**:
The wars interrupted commerce with England, pushing Scots to seek other markets, possibly in continental Europe or Scandinavia. Over the long run, this diversification may have stimulated economic resilience, although the immediate effect was hardship for many.

---

12. Legacy of Wallace, Bruce, and the Independence Struggle

When historians and storytellers recall Scotland's medieval past, the Wars of Independence loom large. William Wallace's bold stand against English occupation, culminating in Stirling Bridge, gave the first spark of widespread revolt. Though he died a brutal death, his spirit of defiance survived in legend, inspiring later generations.

Robert the Bruce built upon Wallace's legacy, forging alliances among nobles and clan leaders, and eventually leading Scotland to victory at Bannockburn. He combined military skill, political ruthlessness (as seen in the killing of Comyn), and a vision of an independent Scotland. The Declaration of Arbroath then provided a statement of collective will, articulating a sense that the nation—rather than any one king—should remain free.

Together, Wallace and Bruce became symbols of courage, loyalty to Scotland, and the principle that a people could resist subjugation by a more powerful neighbor. Their examples resonated in Scottish culture and folklore, shaping how the kingdom saw itself in the centuries to follow.

---

13. The Second War of Independence (Brief Overview)

Although the Treaty of Edinburgh-Northampton in 1328 officially recognized Scottish independence, peace did not last. After Robert the Bruce's death in 1329, his young son, David II, faced renewed English aggression, especially once Edward III exerted full power in England. Rival Scottish claimants, like Edward Balliol (son of John Balliol), sought English support to claim the throne.

This second phase of conflict, lasting into the mid-14th century, again tested Scotland's unity. David II eventually went into exile in France at one point. Yet the Scots, under various leaders, continued to fight for sovereignty. Despite captures, ransoms, and internal strife, they managed to preserve the kingdom's independence. By 1357, the Treaty of Berwick effectively settled the immediate disputes, though tensions with England would flare again in later centuries.

While the Second War of Independence is beyond the main scope of this chapter, it underscores that the fight for Scottish self-rule did not end abruptly with Bruce. The seeds planted during Wallace's uprising and Bannockburn's triumph continued to grow, reinforcing a deep-rooted commitment to autonomy that would color Scotland's political identity up through the early modern era.

---

14. Conclusion

Scotland's Wars of Independence were a defining saga in the kingdom's medieval history. Triggered by a royal succession crisis and fueled by Edward I's bid for overlordship, they saw the rise of iconic leaders who united clans, noble families, and ordinary folk in defense of national freedom. William Wallace's early victories and Robert the Bruce's crowning achievement at Bannockburn stand as high points in a long, grueling conflict. These wars battered Scotland, but also forged a collective sense of identity that transcended local rivalries.

By 1328, through the Treaty of Edinburgh–Northampton, Scotland gained formal recognition of its status as an independent kingdom. Although the struggle continued in a second phase and various treaties would be tested, the first Wars of Independence confirmed that Scotland could not be easily absorbed by England. The Declaration of Arbroath's assertion—that the kingdom's liberty was paramount—remained a powerful statement of nationhood.

In future periods, Scotland would face new challenges: dynastic unions, further feudal reforms, religious upheavals, and shifting European alliances. Yet the memory of Wallace, Bruce, and the Wars of Independence would stay alive in the land's folk memory, shaping how Scots saw their place in the British Isles and the broader medieval world.

CHAPTER 11

ROBERT THE BRUCE AND THE STRUGGLE FOR POWER

1. Introduction

In Chapter 10, we covered Scotland's Wars of Independence, a time of tumult shaped by William Wallace, King John Balliol, and the intrusion of Edward I of England. We also saw Robert the Bruce play a major part in securing Scottish independence, particularly through his crowning achievement at Bannockburn in 1314. This chapter will now focus on Robert the Bruce in more detail—tracing his family background, the rivalries that forced him to fight for his throne, the governance methods he employed once in power, and how his leadership profoundly changed Scotland's political structures.

Though Bruce's military victories are well known, he was more than just a battlefield commander. He built alliances with local lords, refined Scotland's administration, and reached out to continental powers to bolster his legitimacy. By examining these aspects of his reign, we will gain a clearer sense of the complexities underlying medieval kingship in Scotland. We will also delve into how Bruce's rise related to broader European events, such as shifting Anglo-French rivalries and papal politics. In doing so, we see Bruce as a canny statesman, not merely a heroic warrior.

---

2. Bruce's Family Background and Early Ambitions

Long before Robert the Bruce laid claim to the Scottish throne, his family played a significant role in the kingdom's politics. The Bruces (originally de Brus) came from a lineage partly tied to Norman ancestors who had secured lands in both England and Scotland. Through strategic marriages and royal favor, they accumulated estates in Annandale (in southwestern Scotland) and also held properties across northern England. This dual identity was common among high-ranking nobles in the Anglo-Scottish border regions.

Robert the Bruce (b. 1274) thus grew up amid a web of allegiances. His paternal family had once advanced claims to the Scottish throne during the Great Cause of the early 1290s, and his maternal connections (through the earls of Carrick) gave him influence in southwestern Scotland. Politically, he was well-placed to become a contender if a power vacuum arose.

In his youth, Bruce observed the tensions caused by Edward I's overlordship demands. Although we do not have full records of his early education, sources suggest he was multilingual, adept in Norman French (the language of many nobles), possibly Latin for church and legal matters, and of course Scots (either the early Scots tongue or Gaelic influences, depending on the region). This linguistic ability helped him navigate a fractured political scene—where alliances could shift quickly. By the time the Wars of Independence began in 1296, Bruce had inherited or stood in line for significant lands, making him a figure of considerable promise and risk in Edward's eyes.

3. The Complex Years of Loyalty and Rivalry (1296–1306)

Between the outbreak of war (1296) and Bruce's coronation (1306), a decade of shifting alliances tested his political cunning. He sometimes appeared to support the English side, swearing fealty to Edward I in order to preserve his family's lands. Yet he also had private conversations or deals with Scottish leaders who yearned for independence. This dual strategy may appear contradictory by modern standards, but it was not uncommon among medieval nobles who owned cross-border estates. They sought to protect their properties and gauge which faction might eventually prevail.

A prime adversary was John Comyn ("the Red Comyn"), whose family also had a claim to the throne through descent from King Donald III and other lines. Comyn's power base lay in the northeast (Buchan) and in parts of the central Highlands. While Bruce's southwestern block was formidable, the Comyns boasted broad influence, controlling a network of relatives and allied clans. Both Bruce and Comyn recognized that only one of them could become the undisputed leader of the independence cause—if, indeed, the Scots were to break free from English overlordship at all.

As the Wars of Independence advanced, Edward I methodically occupied Scottish strongholds, forcing local lords to submit. Bruce attempted to remain on good terms with the English king while quietly maintaining contact with nationalistic Scots. Such maneuvering put him at constant risk of being branded a traitor by both sides. The turning point arrived in 1306, when Bruce confronted Comyn in the Greyfriars church at Dumfries. Their feud, long simmering, erupted violently, with Comyn mortally wounded. Though details are murky, Bruce realized at that moment he had crossed a line from which there was no return. He seized the moment to claim the throne.

4. Crowning at Scone and Immediate Challenges

Bruce's coronation took place on 25 March 1306 at Scone, the traditional site of Scottish royal inaugurations. The ceremony was hasty because Edward I, once informed of Comyn's death and Bruce's revolt, would undoubtedly move fast. Despite the rushed nature of events, certain symbols of kingship were maintained. Bruce wore a makeshift crown, probably not the original Scottish regalia Edward I had confiscated years before. Isabella MacDuff, Countess of Buchan (from a family typically aligned with the Comyns), controversially sided with Bruce and placed the crown on his head—reflecting an ancient custom that the MacDuffs had the right to enthrone the King of Scots.

This act of crowning Bruce was charged with symbolism. He declared himself the legitimate monarch and thereby invalidated Edward I's position as overlord. Yet Bruce's immediate reality was grim. Many powerful lords still preferred the Comyn alliance or sought Edward's backing. Within weeks, the newly crowned king faced an English army at the Battle of Methven (June 1306). Outnumbered and unprepared, Bruce's forces were routed. He fled to the west, losing key allies along the way. Edward I's lieutenants captured members of Bruce's family, subjecting some to brutal punishment. Even Isabella MacDuff was imprisoned in an open cage, an example of Edward's wrath.

Over the winter of 1306-1307, Bruce survived in hiding, possibly on Rathlin Island off the Irish coast, or moving among sympathetic Highland clans.

Medieval chroniclers include legends of Bruce drawing inspiration from the persistence of a spider weaving its web—though the authenticity of that tale is debated, the story highlights how Scots later romanticized his struggle during those dark months. If any glimmer of hope existed for Bruce, it came in early 1307 when Edward I died, leaving the English throne to the less capable Edward II.

5. Gradual Recovery and the Turn of Fortune (1307–1309)

Edward II lacked his father's forceful leadership, and was soon distracted by tensions within his own baronage. This gave Bruce room to breathe. Re-entering southwestern Scotland, he staged a series of guerrilla attacks that systematically dismantled English garrisons. Slowly, local clans accepted his rule, seeing that Bruce was resilient and that Edward II seemed uncommitted to a massive reconquest. Meanwhile, Bruce's circle of supporters included skilled captains such as James Douglas, Thomas Randolph, and others who would later become linchpins of his army.

By 1308, Bruce turned north to confront rival Scottish families—especially the Comyns. He recognized that unless he subdued these powerful lords, his kingship would remain tenuous. Campaigns in the north were harsh, culminating in the so-called "Harrying of Buchan," where Bruce's forces ravaged Comyn lands, effectively crippling that family's power base. Though medieval warfare was often brutal, this campaign had a particularly devastating effect on the region, indicating that Bruce would not tolerate any further internal opposition.

By early 1309, enough Scottish nobles had rallied to Bruce that he held a parliament in St. Andrews. The gathered lords proclaimed him the legitimate King of Scots, denouncing Edward II's overlordship. Although the struggle was far from over, Bruce had established a functioning government with support across much of the realm. He worked to rebuild local administration, appointing sheriffs and officials loyal to his cause. This consolidation went hand in hand with efforts to secure foreign recognition, as Bruce understood that diplomatic ties could strengthen Scotland's position.

6. Foreign Diplomacy and the Auld Alliance

An essential aspect of Bruce's strategy was aligning with France, a perennial rival of England. Earlier, King John Balliol and his supporters had pursued ties with the French court, but Bruce aimed to deepen and formalize these connections. France, embroiled in repeated conflicts with England, found common interest in supporting the Scots. Over time, what became known as the "Auld Alliance" took shape—a Franco-Scottish pact that promised military and political cooperation against England.

Though Bruce did not conclusively finalize the terms we see in later centuries, his overtures to the French king paved the way for shipments of arms, supplies, or safe harbor for Scottish envoys. At times, French diplomats mediated with the papacy on Bruce's behalf, seeking papal recognition of his crown. Papal support was crucial: if the Pope accepted Bruce as the rightful King of Scots, it weakened Edward II's claims of feudal superiority.

Still, the church was cautious. Edward I had once manipulated ecclesiastical authorities to back English claims, and popes typically avoided offending powerful monarchs. Yet as English politics grew unstable under Edward II, and as Bruce's cause demonstrated greater unity, the papacy gradually leaned towards acknowledging Scottish independence. This slow shift in international legitimacy paralleled Bruce's military gains at home, culminating in a stronger moral and legal foundation for his reign.

7. The Road to Bannockburn

Although Robert the Bruce had secured much of Scotland by 1313, key strongholds remained under English control—most prominently Stirling Castle, a strategic fortress near the River Forth that guarded central routes. Stirling had symbolic and tactical value for both sides. In 1313, Bruce's brother Edward led a siege and forced an agreement that if an English relief army did not arrive by Midsummer Day 1314, the garrison would surrender the castle to Bruce.

Edward II, eager to redeem his father's legacy and to prevent the fall of Stirling, marched north in the summer of 1314 with a large force. Bruce, anticipating this move, gathered his own forces near the Bannock Burn, a stream that flowed through marshy terrain not far from Stirling. The Scots, though outnumbered, selected ground advantageous for infantry. On the first day of skirmishing (23 June 1314), Scottish spearmen repulsed English cavalry attacks. The second day (24 June) saw a full-scale English assault that devolved into panic when the Scottish schiltrons held firm and the narrow battleground prevented English knights from maneuvering effectively.

The victory at Bannockburn was overwhelming. Edward II fled, leaving many of his top nobles captured or killed. News of Bannockburn electrified Europe, demonstrating that Bruce's monarchy was far from a mere rebellion. Overnight, Bruce's prestige soared, while Edward II's credibility plummeted. Although the war would continue in fits and starts, the result at Bannockburn effectively ensured that Bruce's rule could not be undone by force of arms.

8. Governing Scotland in the Wake of Victory

Even though Bannockburn was a massive triumph, Robert the Bruce faced the challenge of rebuilding a country ravaged by years of war. Many regions, especially border areas and the northeast, had suffered repeated clashes. Castles needed repair or demolition (in some cases, Bruce ordered the slighting of certain castles to prevent them from falling back into enemy hands). Local economies had to recover from disruptions to trade and agriculture.

Administration under Bruce balanced feudal norms with the particularities of Scottish custom. He re-granted lands to loyal supporters, a process that reshaped the nobility. Clans that had resisted him were stripped of estates, while new families, or older families that had proven their loyalty, received titles. This reorganization fostered strong bonds between Bruce and his aristocracy, creating a network of mutual support. It also meant that Bruce's monarchy became tied to certain influential clans, setting precedents for how future kings would handle noble patronage.

The Church cooperated closely. Clerics who supported Bruce were rewarded with ecclesiastical positions, and monastic houses that had suffered under English occupancy regained privileges. Bruce, for his part, saw the Church as a stabilizing institution that could legitimize his reign in the eyes of the populace. Sermons from the pulpit, blessings of banners, and written chronicles describing Bruce as a God-given leader all helped reinforce his authority.

9. The Declaration of Arbroath and Papal Recognition

To further secure international recognition, the Scots penned the Declaration of Arbroath in 1320, a letter addressed to Pope John XXII. While Chapter 10 briefly noted its significance, here we consider how it fits into Bruce's broader effort to maintain unity and project a vision of Scottish independence. Composed in Latin, the declaration famously stated that if Robert the Bruce failed to defend Scotland's freedom, the nobles would choose another king—a remarkable statement of conditional loyalty.

Though historians debate the practical impact of the Declaration of Arbroath at the time, it clearly expressed the kingdom's collective desire to remain free from English domination. Robert the Bruce's cause, framed as a national struggle with strong noble consensus, gained moral weight. The Pope, initially hesitant, began stepping away from Edward II's line. By the mid-1320s, Bruce's position was strong enough that even some English magnates questioned the wisdom of continued warfare, especially given Edward II's troubled reign and feuds with his own barons.

10. The Treaty of Edinburgh-Northampton (1328)

Ultimately, English acceptance of Bruce's kingship came in 1328 with the Treaty of Edinburgh-Northampton, signed under the regency government of Queen Isabella (Edward II's wife) and Roger Mortimer during the minority of Edward III. This treaty recognized Scotland's sovereignty and Robert the Bruce as its king. The English also agreed to return the Scottish regalia and other seized items—though the Stone of Destiny (also called the Stone of Scone) was never given back at that time.

Bruce, in turn, consented to a royal marriage between his son David (the future David II) and Edward III's sister Joan, forging a bond that aimed to stabilize the two kingdoms' relations. While many English lords despised the treaty as humiliating, it was a formal acknowledgment that Bruce had succeeded in his quest for independence. The arrangement did not bring everlasting peace, but it solidified Bruce's achievements.

---

11. The Final Years of Robert the Bruce

By the time of the treaty, Robert the Bruce was in declining health. Contemporary sources suggest he suffered from a serious ailment, possibly leprosy. Despite his condition, he continued to govern with the help of close advisors. In his final months, Bruce focused on securing the succession of his young son David, ensuring that loyal guardians would guide the boy-king if Bruce died prematurely.

Robert the Bruce passed away in June 1329 at the age of 54 or 55. According to popular tradition, he requested that his heart be taken on a crusade to the Holy Land, though in practice it ended up traveling to Spain with Sir James Douglas to fight against the Moors. Bruce's remains were interred at Dunfermline Abbey, a royal mausoleum site. Over centuries, his gravesite became a place of reverence, though repeated expansions and later disruptions sometimes obscured the exact burial. Nonetheless, Bruce's memory endured as the champion-king who reclaimed Scotland's independence.

---

12. Bruce's Broader Impact on the Scottish Monarchy

Robert the Bruce's legacy extends well beyond Bannockburn or the Declaration of Arbroath. He fundamentally reshaped the monarchy, establishing precedents for how a king could unify fragmented nobility through both patronage and force. He also emphasized the importance of forging ties with Europe's major powers—especially France and, indirectly, the papacy—thereby integrating Scotland into continental diplomacy.

Administration under Bruce showcased a blend of Gaelic traditions (like clan leadership and local assemblies) with feudal structures that had intensified since the Norman influence. The reorganization of noble lands created a new aristocratic order, one bound by loyalty to Bruce's lineage. This pattern would influence subsequent generations, making the monarchy more reliant on alliances with powerful lords who traced their fortunes back to Bruce's patronage.

Bruce's success also underscored the power of collective identity. While medieval Scotland remained an assortment of dialects, clans, and local customs, the Wars of Independence had fostered a sense of national unity. This cohesion, nurtured by Bruce's skillful leadership, would help Scotland weather additional storms, such as the second phase of the Independence Wars under David II and future disputes with the English crown.

---

13. Contrasts with Other Medieval Rulers

Comparing Robert the Bruce's reign to other European monarchs of the era highlights certain distinctive features:

- **Ruthless Consolidation**: Like many kings, Bruce did not hesitate to deal harshly with enemies. Yet the scale of internal conflict—his personal slaying of Comyn in a church and subsequent "Harrying of Buchan"—was stark. Still, such acts were not far removed from standard medieval power struggles, where eliminating rivals was a harsh necessity.
- **Reliance on Loyal Lieutenants**: Whereas some monarchs tried to maintain broad, superficial alliances, Bruce built a core group of faithful captains: James "the Black" Douglas, Thomas Randolph (Earl of Moray), and others. This cadre functioned almost like a familial retinue, echoing the Gaelic concept of a chief surrounded by his band of warrior companions.
- **National Inspiration**: Few medieval kings so deeply captured the imagination of their people as Bruce did in Scotland. His personal

saga—ranging from defeat and exile to glorious victory—became symbolic of the entire kingdom's resilience. Even centuries later, Scots invoked Bruce's name to rally unity.
- **Strategic Diplomacy**: Bruce's international maneuvers with the papacy and France reveal a shrewd awareness of how to leverage external powers. This combination of domestic might and foreign support was a hallmark of stable medieval kingship, allowing smaller realms to survive amid bigger rivals.

14. Transitioning to the Post-Bruce Era

Bruce's death in 1329 thrust Scotland into a new phase, often called the Second War of Independence, as Edward III, once he came of age, sought to regain influence. Bruce's son, David II, only five years old at his father's passing, depended on guardians who tried to uphold Bruce's legacy. In the immediate aftermath, factions emerged, including supporters of Edward Balliol (the son of John Balliol), who contested the throne with English backing. This new conflict repeated certain patterns from Bruce's earlier struggles, though the personalities and alliances had shifted.

Nonetheless, Bruce's achievements were not easily undone. The major families he had elevated remained vital players, resisting English invasions and asserting Scottish sovereignty. His memory and the institutional frameworks he left behind offered a rallying point for those determined to keep Scotland independent. Even though David II faced captivity and internal strife, the kingdom survived. By the mid-14th century, many recognized that Robert the Bruce had laid deep foundations for Scottish monarchy.

15. Conclusion

Robert the Bruce is remembered as one of Scotland's most iconic monarchs, yet his path to power was fraught with moral dilemmas, violent rivalries, and shifting loyalties. Emerging from a family with cross-border estates, he navigated the chaotic aftermath of the Great Cause, contended with the Comyn faction, and ultimately seized the throne by force in 1306. His early defeats drove him into hiding, but Edward I's death in 1307 and Bruce's resilience flipped his fortunes.

Through determined guerrilla warfare, strategic alliances, and a merciless crackdown on internal foes, Bruce restored Scottish governance under his leadership. Bannockburn (1314) became his crowning victory, bolstering his position domestically and earning him a heroic reputation. Diplomatic efforts, exemplified by the Declaration of Arbroath and alignment with France, secured papal and international acknowledgment. By 1328, the Treaty of Edinburgh–Northampton sealed Scotland's independence with English recognition.

Bruce's reforms shaped the medieval Scottish monarchy, intertwining Gaelic clan structures with the feudalism that had taken root. His distribution of lands strengthened loyal families and redefined the noble hierarchy for decades. Beyond immediate politics, Bruce's story resonated as a testament to Scotland's capacity for unity and national identity in the face of a more powerful neighbor. That legacy would persist in later centuries, influencing how Scots saw themselves and their kings long after Robert the Bruce's death.

CHAPTER 12

THE STEWART DYNASTY TAKES SHAPE

1. Introduction

Following Robert the Bruce's transformative reign, Scotland continued wrestling with political upheavals and renewed English aggression. By the mid-14th century, the Bruce lineage faced challenges, leading the crown eventually to pass to the Stewarts. Also spelled "Stewart" or "Stuart," this family rose from relatively humble beginnings as hereditary High Stewards of Scotland to become the ruling dynasty. Their ascent marked a new chapter in Scottish governance—one that combined Gaelic, Norman, and Bruce-era influences into a more formalized royal tradition.

In this chapter, we will trace how the Stewarts secured the throne, examining figures like Robert II and Robert III, as well as the intricate power dynamics they faced. We will look at how the monarchy navigated internal noble rivalries, the enduring tension with England, the progression of royal institutions, and the deepening cultural shift toward Lowland governance. As the Stewarts established themselves, they laid foundations for the medieval Scottish state that would ultimately face fresh religious and political storms in later centuries.

---

2. Background: The Post-Bruce Succession and David II

David briefly considered naming Edward III or one of Edward's sons as heir—a shocking prospect that risked returning Scotland to a subordinate status under English rule. The very idea outraged many Scottish lords, who had sacrificed much to maintain their kingdom's independence during the Wars of Independence. Ultimately, David abandoned that plan, understanding it would cause widespread rebellion.

By the late 1360s, David II's fragile health and lack of an heir grew more pressing. Nobles began looking to the closest royal relatives from the extended Bruce family tree. That lineage included the descendants of

Marjorie Bruce, Robert the Bruce's daughter, who had married Walter, the sixth High Steward of Scotland. Their son, Robert Stewart, thus carried Bruce blood through his mother, while also inheriting the influential office of High Steward from his father's side. If David II died childless, Robert Stewart was widely recognized as the next in line.

Though King David II occasionally feuded with Robert Stewart—particularly during the king's captivity—circumstances kept pointing to Robert as the eventual successor. As David's reign wore on, the realm needed a stable plan for the future. The Scottish Parliament and key magnates signaled their support for Robert Stewart's claim, viewing him as someone who could uphold the legacy of Robert the Bruce while keeping Scotland independent from England.

In 1371, King David II passed away, leaving no direct heirs. The crown, by birthright and parliamentary acceptance, fell to Robert Stewart, who ascended the throne as **Robert II**, the first Stewart (or "Stuart") king of Scotland. This moment stands as a major turning point: the end of the Bruce direct line and the formal rise of the Stewart dynasty that would preside over Scotland for centuries to come.

---

3. The High Stewardship and the Stewart Family's Rise

Before exploring Robert II's reign, it is worth understanding the Stewart family background. The hereditary post of High Steward began with David I (r. 1124–1153), who appointed a trusted figure to oversee royal estates and manage the king's household. Over generations, the Stewards (later spelled "Stewart" or "Stuart") increased their wealth and influence through successful administration, political marriages, and land acquisitions. The office gave them direct access to the monarch's inner circle, allowing them to weave alliances with major lords.

Walter, the sixth High Steward, married Marjorie Bruce, daughter of Robert the Bruce. This marriage bound the Stewarts to the royal line. Their son, Robert Stewart (later Robert II), was born around 1316. From childhood, Robert was positioned among the highest nobility, bridging the gap between the old Gaelic aristocracy and the Norman-influenced families that had emerged under David I and subsequent kings. During David II's minority and exile, Robert Stewart sometimes acted as a regent, building further ties with regional magnates and strengthening his family's credibility as potential royal successors.

By the time he took the throne, Robert II was about 55 years old—relatively advanced in age for a new king. Despite concerns over his vigor, his extensive network and experience in governance made him a unifying figure. To many, Robert II represented a safe choice who combined the Bruce heritage with the practical know-how of the steward's office.

4. Reign of Robert II (1371–1390): Balancing Old and New

Upon coronation in 1371, Robert II inherited a kingdom still cautious of English ambitions, yet also grappling with internal regional tensions. With the ongoing Hundred Years' War (1337–1453) between England and France, Scotland maintained the "Auld Alliance" with the French kingdom—a partnership that could provide military and economic advantages. However, Robert II faced challenges on multiple fronts:

1. **Noble Power Blocks**
    - Major families such as the Douglases, the Dunbars, and the MacDonalds (Lords of the Isles) held large territories, sometimes acting with near-royal authority in their domains. Robert II had to negotiate with them, granting favors or titles in return for loyalty.
2. **Border Raids and Anglo-Scottish Skirmishes**
    - The border region between Scotland and England, known as the Marches, remained volatile. Raids, retaliations, and shifting truces continued to disrupt trade and agriculture. Robert II tried to manage local wardens (powerful lords responsible for defending the frontier) to avoid open warfare with England, while still asserting Scottish claims to certain contested lands.
3. **Royal Administration**
    - Robert II's personal style leaned toward delegation. He preferred to rule through a council of trusted nobles and

kin, rather than imposing direct royal power. Some saw this as wise consensus-building; others complained he was too passive. Over time, his sons and leading magnates assumed key roles in governance, shaping a quasi-collective monarchy.

4. **Dynastic Security**
    - Unlike David II, Robert II fathered numerous children, ensuring a strong Stewart line. He had married Elizabeth Mure (recognized officially after some initial questions over the legality of their union) and later Euphemia de Ross. Through these marriages, he produced a large brood of sons and daughters. This proliferation of heirs both stabilized succession and sowed seeds for future rivalries among Stewart princes.

Despite occasional criticisms that Robert II was not an energetic king, Scotland saw relative peace compared to the tumultuous eras of the Wars of Independence. Small-scale border wars flared, but no catastrophic invasion like those under Edward I occurred. By carefully balancing noble interests, Robert II held the realm together, albeit with less personal authority than some predecessors. He died in 1390, leaving the crown to his son John, who took the regnal name **Robert III** in deference to the memory of Robert the Bruce.

---

5. Robert III (1390–1406): Challenges and Noble Dominance

John Stewart's decision to rule as Robert III signaled his wish to align with the great hero-king's legacy. Yet Robert III faced major obstacles:

- **Personal Frailty**:
    - He had suffered an injury, possibly from a horse kick, that left him physically weak. Some chroniclers suggest he also lacked strong confidence or a forceful character. As a result, Robert III struggled to assert control over ambitious nobles.
- **Power of the Duke of Albany**:

- - Robert III's younger brother, Robert Stewart, Duke of Albany, rose to command much of the kingdom's day-to-day governance. Albany was shrewd and politically adept. Many suspected he aimed to govern Scotland in all but name, overshadowing the king.
  - This created a tense dynamic within the royal family. While Robert III theoretically held the throne, Albany managed much of the practical administration.
- **England and Border Issues**:
  - England's King Richard II had his own internal crises, followed by the Lancastrian takeover by Henry IV in 1399. Anglo-Scottish relations remained tense. The Scots occasionally supported English rebels, and cross-border raids continued. Robert III could do little to unify a strong foreign policy, given his diminished authority at court.
- **Clan Tensions in the Highlands**:
  - The Lords of the Isles (the MacDonald family) wielded near-autonomous power over the Hebrides and large swaths of the western Highlands. They might ally with or oppose the crown depending on local interests. Robert III, overshadowed by Albany, found it difficult to impose direct royal rule in these distant regions.
  - Infighting between clans, such as the MacDonalds and the Camerons or Mackenzies, required careful mediation. The king's limited presence allowed regional magnates to pursue their own agendas.

Frustrated by his brother's dominance, Robert III tried to strengthen his son, Prince David (Duke of Rothesay), giving him responsibilities to overshadow Albany. But the experiment ended tragically: Duke of Rothesay died in suspicious circumstances (1402) while under Albany's "protective custody" at Falkland Palace. Many suspected foul play, though direct proof never emerged. After losing his heir, a grief-stricken Robert III saw the monarchy's weakness laid bare.

Fearing for his younger son James's safety, Robert III sent him to France in 1406. English pirates captured James en route, delivering him to King Henry IV. When Robert III heard of his son's capture, he reputedly died of despair. The king's death that same year left Scotland in Albany's hands once more—since James, the new king (James I), languished as a hostage in England.

6. Regency of the Duke of Albany and the Stewart State

With James I a prisoner in England, Robert Stewart, Duke of Albany, served as regent (1406–1420). His rule was effectively that of a king, minus the title. Albany solidified alliances with leading magnates, further entrenching noble autonomy. While he maintained the Stewart name on the throne, he had little incentive to pay James's ransom promptly; a child king in captivity posed no threat to Albany's dominance.

Meanwhile, the kingdom functioned through local aristocrats. The Highlands remained fractious, with clan battles flaring. The Lords of the Isles occasionally tested the regent's authority. In the Lowlands, the Douglas family grew ever stronger, expanding their estates and forging ties with continental powers. Some historians argue that Albany allowed these magnates free rein as long as they recognized his regency.

Despite these issues, Albany kept Scotland relatively stable. He negotiated truces with England, albeit short-lived, and managed to keep real civil war at bay. Taxes remained moderate since the monarchy did not fund large-scale campaigns. The economy slowly recovered from earlier devastations. Still, the monarchy's prestige waned. Many Scots yearned for the rightful king to return and take personal control of royal governance.

When Robert, Duke of Albany, died in 1420, his son Murdoch inherited the regency. Murdoch lacked his father's skill, facing criticism from nobles who blamed him for failing to secure James's release. Under Murdoch, mismanagement and conflict intensified, setting the stage for the eventual homecoming of James I in 1424—a moment that would drastically alter the Stewart monarchy's trajectory.

7. James I Returns: Restoring Royal Authority (1424–1437)

Finally released after extended negotiations and a ransom payment, James I returned to Scotland at age 30 in 1424. He had spent many formative years in England, absorbing aspects of English court life, administration, and possibly the English language in its higher forms. This background gave him a unique perspective—he was a Scottish king with an English-style education, determined to reassert strong royal power after decades of regency rule.

James I wasted no time:

1. **Reining in Over-Mighty Nobles**
   - Suspicious of those who had flourished during his captivity, James targeted leading families associated with the Albany regents. He arrested Murdoch, Duke of Albany, along with several relatives. They were tried on charges of treason and executed in 1425. This dramatic purge signaled the end of the "Albany era."
   - James also reclaimed estates, reorganized regional power structures, and introduced new royal officials. He aimed to create a centralized administration loyal to the crown, not just local lords.
2. **Judicial and Financial Reforms**
   - Determined to modernize governance, James I expanded the use of general councils and parliament. He focused on standardizing measures and coinage.
   - Laws were passed to curb corruption among sheriffs and to regulate the conduct of courts, reflecting an attempt to impose a "king's justice" across all shires.
3. **Relations with England**
   - James I initially maintained a cautious peace with England. He recognized that Scotland could not afford a prolonged war given the heavy ransom debt still owed for his release. The Hundred Years' War, still raging between England and France, made Scotland's foreign policy delicate. James strove to uphold the Auld Alliance while avoiding direct confrontation.
4. **Church and Cultural Initiatives**

- Like earlier Stewart and Bruce monarchs, James cultivated strong ties with the clergy. Monastic patronage, foundations, and endowments helped secure church support.
- Cultural projects, such as supporting poets or hosting more refined court ceremonies, elevated the monarchy's image. Some chroniclers praise James I for a revival of learning, though actual literacy rates among nobles remained limited.

Although James I stabilized the monarchy, his forceful methods and stern taxation to pay the English ransom angered influential families. In 1437, a conspiracy led by the Earl of Atholl's faction assassinated James at the Dominican Friary in Perth. This brutal killing highlighted how swiftly noble resentment could flare into violence. Nevertheless, James I's reign stands out for pushing a more centralized royal agenda, reclaiming authority that had been eroded under the Albany regents.

---

8. Stewart Kings After James I: Continued Struggle and Growth

The subsequent Stewart kings—James II, James III, and James IV—each faced their own challenges but continued the process of consolidating royal authority. Though detailing each reign lies beyond our current chapter's scope, a brief overview will show how the Stewart line evolved:

1. **James II (1437–1460)**
   - Only six when his father was assassinated, James II grew up under regencies and factional guardians. Once of age, he tried to curb powerful barons like the Black Douglases. His reign was marked by battles and negotiations aimed at reining in over-mighty subjects, echoing James I's policies.
   - Known for modernizing Scotland's artillery—he acquired huge cannons, including the famous "Mons Meg"—James II died in 1460 at the Siege of Roxburgh Castle, reportedly when one of his cannons exploded.
2. **James III (1460–1488)**

- Surrounded by intrigues, James III had a more cautious and sometimes unpopular style. He quarreled with his own siblings and faced revolts from nobles who saw him as too aloof or influenced by unpopular favorites at court.
- In 1488, James III was killed at the Battle of Sauchieburn, possibly by rebellious nobles. His teenage son, James IV, then ascended to the throne.

3. **James IV (1488–1513)**
    - Widely regarded as a dynamic and charismatic king, James IV improved the navy, built strong government institutions, and patronized the arts, earning admiration at home and abroad.
    - His downfall came at the Battle of Flodden (1513) against England's Henry VIII, where James IV and much of the Scottish nobility perished, shaking the country deeply.

These patterns of ambition, noble opposition, and occasional royal triumph underscored the Stewart monarchy's fragile dance with Scotland's powerful aristocratic families. Despite repeated crises, the Stewart line secured the throne for generations, further defining Scotland's medieval identity.

---

9. The Medieval Stewart State: Themes and Institutions

By the later 15th century, one could speak of a more cohesive "Stewart state" in Scotland. Several factors shaped its medieval character:

1. **Royal Parliament and Councils**
    - Building on earlier precedents, the Stewart kings continued to convene parliaments where bishops, abbots, earls, and barons gathered. While not a parliament in the modern sense, it served as a forum for negotiating taxes, passing laws, and settling disputes.
    - Lesser councils met frequently, advising the king on justice, foreign policy, and feudal grants.
2. **Feudalism and Land Grants**
    - Like their predecessors, Stewart kings used land patronage to reward loyal lords or gain new supporters. The

Douglases, Hamiltons, Gordons, and other major families expanded through royal charters.
   - Yet the crown also faced the risk that any single family might become too powerful, leading to periodic royal clampdowns.
3. **Church Influence**
   - The Church in Scotland continued to function as an essential pillar of monarchy. Bishops and abbots were often from noble families, intertwining ecclesiastical and secular power. Church-endowed institutions—like the University of St Andrews (founded 1413)—arose, fostering some scholarship and literacy within the kingdom's elites.
4. **Clan Dynamics**
   - In the Highlands and Isles, clan organization remained paramount. The Lords of the Isles at times acted almost like independent monarchs. Even after the crown worked to reduce their power, conflicts among Highland clans required ongoing royal mediation.
   - The gap between the Gaelic-speaking Highlands and the more "feudalized," Scots-speaking Lowlands persisted. The Stewarts oversaw an ever-deepening cultural and linguistic divide, even as they strove to claim authority over all Scots.
5. **Urban Growth and Commerce**
   - Towns like Edinburgh, Perth, Dundee, and Aberdeen grew as centers for trade and crafts. Burghs received royal charters, encouraging merchants to form guilds and conduct commerce with the Low Countries, Germany, or France.
   - This modest economic development helped the monarchy collect taxes, though revenue remained far less than that of England or major continental states.

Overall, the Stewart state was not as centralized as, say, France under the Capetian or Valois kings. It remained a patchwork of local powers loosely held together. Nonetheless, compared to the chaotic 14th century, the 15th-century Stewart realm was more structurally sound, with deeper royal institutions that survived kingly minorities or occasional internal rebellions.

10. Cultural Flourishing and Ties to Europe

During the Stewart ascendancy, Scotland's ties to continental Europe reinforced both its political strategies and cultural blossoming:

- **Auld Alliance**
    - Military cooperation continued with France against England. Royal marriages frequently connected Scottish and French nobles, further mingling aristocratic lineages. Some Scottish lords, and even common soldiers, served in French armies.
    - French architectural and artistic influences arrived with returning soldiers or traveling envoys, evident in the stylings of some royal residences.
- **Literature and Courtly Life**
    - The Stewart court patronized poets and chroniclers, leading to works that celebrated the monarchy's exploits and genealogies. Figures like the poet Robert Henryson wrote moral fables and sophisticated verse in the Scots language, reflecting a literate environment that appealed to nobles.
    - King James I himself was credited (perhaps apocryphally) with authoring "The Kingis Quair," a poem expressing courtly love and personal reflection. True or not, such tales built a legend of royal involvement in the arts.
- **Diplomatic Marriages**
    - To strengthen the monarchy's standing, Stewart kings often married into foreign noble families. James II wed Mary of Guelders (from the Netherlands region), James III married Margaret of Denmark, and James IV famously married Margaret Tudor of England (in 1503), paving the way for the later union of crowns.

In these ways, the Stewart dynasty integrated Scotland into broader European currents, fostering a sense of connection that transcended insular clan disputes. While these continental links did not erase tensions at home, they enriched the cultural tapestry of medieval Scotland.

11. Persistent Challenges: Noble Revolts and Border Hostility

Despite the Stewarts' overall consolidation, the monarchy faced recurrent challenges:

- **Noble Revolts**
    - Time and again, major barons or alliances of lords rebelled when they felt threatened by royal attempts to curb their power. For instance, repeated conflicts with the Black Douglases in the 15th century ended with the Douglases' downfall, but only after a series of violent confrontations.
- **Border Warfare**
    - While large-scale invasions by English kings were less frequent than in the days of Edward I or Edward II, the border remained a hotbed of raids (referred to as "rieving"). Wardens of the Marches, both Scottish and English, staged forays into enemy territory to seize cattle and goods, fueling a cycle of revenge.
    - The monarchy tried to negotiate truces or treaties, but these often broke down, especially when local border families—like the Scotts, Kerrs, or Elliots—pursued their own vendettas or alliances.
- **Clan Feuds in the North**
    - The crown's stance toward the Lords of the Isles swung between confrontation and accommodation. By the late 15th century, the monarchy took steps to dismantle the MacDonalds' autonomy, culminating in the forfeiture of the Lordship of the Isles in 1493 under James IV. Still, unrest flared repeatedly, requiring royal expeditions into the Highlands.

Such turmoil meant that, even under Stewart rule, Scotland's monarchy had to balance force with diplomacy, forging ever-shifting coalitions to keep the realm intact. The king's success depended on personal leadership, cunning in dealing with powerful families, and an underlying network of smaller lairds and burgh officials who kept local economies running.

12. Social Transformations Under the Early Stewarts

While the earlier medieval period revolved around a rural, clan-based economy, changes during the Stewart era gradually transformed society:

1. **Growth of Towns and Guilds**
    - Increasing trade with Flanders and other North Sea regions spurred the rise of Scottish burghs. Urban populations expanded, though never reaching the scale of major continental cities. Craftsmen formed guilds (e.g., smiths, weavers, merchants) that regulated standards and training.
    - Town councils, authorized by royal charter, gained a degree of self-governance. They collected tolls, enforced local laws, and contributed taxes to the crown.
2. **Knighthood and Heraldry**
    - Influenced by European chivalric culture, many Scottish nobles adopted coats of arms and seals, demonstrating lineage pride. Tournaments and jousts, though not as common as in England or France, emerged as displays of noble prestige.
    - Heraldic traditions were regulated to an extent, with certain offices dedicated to recording arms and genealogies.
3. **Peasantry and Land Tenure**
    - Most of the population remained peasants living on estates owned by nobles, the Church, or the crown. Feudal dues and rents shaped rural life. Though not free in the modern sense, many peasants had limited autonomy to farm their strips of land as long as they paid their obligations.
    - In the Borders and Highlands, some communities operated under looser clan systems, blending feudal obligations with Gaelic customs. Ties of kinship and loyalty to a chief often superseded formal feudal structures.
4. **Religion and Parish Life**
    - The Church, with its network of parishes, monasteries, and cathedrals, was central to social life. Holy days punctuated

the calendar, offering respite from labor and uniting communities in religious festivals.
    - Pilgrimages to local shrines (like St. Ninian's at Whithorn) or to more distant sites reaffirmed spiritual bonds. At the same time, ecclesiastical courts handled marriage disputes, moral offenses, and other issues that spilled over from secular law.

Overall, while the Stewart era did not revolutionize everyday life, it gradually nudged Scotland toward more structured governance, deeper engagement in North Sea and European trade, and increased reliance on written charters and records. The monarchy's fortunes grew tied to urban merchants and lesser lairds, even as old feudal ties still bound them to great magnates.

---

13. The Stewart Dynasty's Medieval Legacy

By the dawn of the 16th century, the Stewart dynasty had firmly planted its roots. This legacy, intertwined with the memory of Robert the Bruce, shaped Scotland's political culture:

1. **Continued Royal Line**
    - The Stewarts never forgot their descent from Marjorie Bruce, frequently invoking that link in official ceremonies. It allowed them to claim continuity from the heroic era of the Wars of Independence.
    - Generations of Stewart heirs gave Scotland a relatively stable line of succession (despite the minority reigns and assassinations). This stability contrasted with earlier periods when the throne changed hands violently or threatened to pass to an English king.
2. **Consolidation of Lowland Control**
    - Over successive reigns, Stewart monarchs expanded direct authority in the Lowlands, establishing a tradition of more centralized rule. They learned to coordinate law courts, parliaments, and local officials to a greater degree than ever before.
3. **Highland Complexity**

- The Highlands and Islands, while never fully subjugated in a modern sense, faced more intervention from the crown, gradually eroding old Gaelic lordships like the MacDonald-held Lordship of the Isles.
- This process was uneven, leaving pockets of fierce autonomy that would later challenge central government in future centuries.

4. **Greater Engagement in European Affairs**
    - Dynastic marriages and alliances carried Scotland into the diplomatic orbit of larger states, especially France. Scottish mercenaries served abroad, and foreign knights visited Scottish courts. The monarchy used these ties to counterbalance English pressure.
    - At the same time, repeated border conflicts with England shaped a martial ethos among the nobility, generating a culture that prized military leadership and frontier resilience.

Thus, the Stewart dynasty set the stage for a medieval kingdom that, while not as populous or wealthy as England or France, possessed distinct institutions and traditions. The memory of independence—rooted in the Bruce era—remained strong, coupled with more refined governance under Stewart kings who straddled the line between clan-based medievalism and emerging centralized feudal states.

---

14. Chapter Summary and Looking Ahead

From the death of David II in 1371 to the advent of James IV in the late 15th century, the Stewart family shaped Scotland's monarchy in crucial ways. Robert II began the dynasty as an older, consensus-focused king, leaving behind a broad Stewart clan that intermarried with leading nobility. Robert III struggled against internal power plays, particularly from his own brother Albany, culminating in the heartbreak of losing his heir and sending his younger son James into captivity.

Under the Albany regencies, the monarchy's authority declined, giving nobles freer rein—until James I returned from English imprisonment in 1424 and launched a forceful program of centralization. His successors, James II and James III, wrestled with powerful lords and border tensions. Each faced rebellions or conspiracies, showing how precarious medieval kingship could be. Still, through determination, alliances, and sometimes ruthless action, the Stewarts embedded themselves at Scotland's helm.

By the close of the 15th century, the Stewart monarchy had achieved notable successes: a functioning parliament, a network of royal officials, and deeper ties to continental Europe. Yet challenges remained—internal factionalism, Gaelic unrest, border hostilities, and competition from mighty neighbors. The stage was set for further evolution under James IV and James V, eventually leading into the Reformation era and beyond. But in purely medieval terms, the Stewart dynasty had taken firm shape, forging a legacy that blended the memory of Bruce with a new royal tradition—one that would endure for centuries and ultimately unite the Scottish and English crowns in a later age.

CHAPTER 13

THE REFORMATION AND RELIGIOUS STRIFE

1. Introduction

By the early 16th century, Scotland was under the rule of the Stewart dynasty, a royal line that had gradually strengthened its power but still contended with influential nobility and deep regional differences. Alongside these political challenges, a major transformation was brewing: the Protestant Reformation. Sparked by theological debates and the spread of new ideas from continental Europe—particularly from Martin Luther's Germany and John Calvin's Geneva—Scotland's population was introduced to criticisms of the Roman Catholic Church. Many Scots found the new doctrines appealing, especially amid concerns about corruption and the wealth of the clergy.

However, this religious upheaval did not occur in a vacuum. The Reformation intersected with Scotland's complex political alliances and rivalries—especially its centuries-old relationship with Catholic France (the "Auld Alliance") and its shifting stance toward Protestant England. This chapter examines how the Reformation entered Scotland, how it stoked conflict among the nobility, and how figures like John Knox shaped the nascent Church of Scotland. We will also see how the resulting religious divisions sparked social unrest, toppled the medieval church structure, and led to enduring transformations that set the stage for future conflicts.

2. Background: A Medieval Church on the Eve of Reform

In the century before the Reformation, the Roman Catholic Church in Scotland held vast landholdings, and its bishops and abbots often came from noble families. As a result, high-ranking clergy wielded both spiritual and temporal power. Monasteries served as centers of learning and charity, while parish churches anchored community religious life. Pilgrimages to shrines—like St. Ninian's at Whithorn or St. Andrews' relics—remained common.

Nevertheless, critics pointed out concerns:

- **Clerical Wealth**: Some bishops and abbots led lavish lifestyles, drawing large incomes from church lands while many ordinary parish priests lived modestly.
- **Pluralism and Absenteeism**: Certain clerics held multiple benefices or rarely visited their assigned parishes, causing resentment.
- **Spiritual Disconnect**: Many laypeople felt a gulf between formal church practices (elaborate Latin masses, indulgences) and simpler personal devotion.

In the late 15th and early 16th centuries, voices calling for reform grew louder across Europe. Even within Scotland, some sought better education for clergy, improved preaching, and an end to abuses. However, the impetus for a radical break with Rome accelerated once Luther's ideas (after 1517) and other Protestant writings arrived. Printed pamphlets circulated despite censorship, eventually capturing the interest of key nobles who saw Protestantism as a way to challenge Catholic France's influence and reduce the Church's wealth.

---

3. Early Protestant Influences in Scotland

During James IV's reign (1488–1513), Scotland maintained a strong Catholic identity. James IV himself was devout, funding church projects and pilgrimages. Still, after his death at the Battle of Flodden (1513), the country entered a period of regencies under James V's minority. Into this uncertain climate came the first wave of Reformation pamphlets and ideas from abroad:

- **Patrick Hamilton**
    - A young scholar influenced by Lutheran thought, Hamilton preached justification by faith. He was arrested under King James V's regime and burned at the stake in 1528. Hamilton became Scotland's first notable Protestant martyr, spurring curiosity about his teachings rather than silencing them.
- **George Wishart**
    - Another preacher, Wishart traveled widely, sharing the New Testament's message in the vernacular. He was executed in

1546, again reinforcing the perception that the established church violently suppressed dissent. Wishart's disciples included John Knox, who would become the foremost leader of the Scottish Reformation.

Throughout James V's adult reign (1528–1542), Scotland aligned with Catholic France, especially through James's marriage to French nobles. The king and his French-born queen, Mary of Guise, opposed Protestant infiltration. Church authorities used heresy trials to stem the tide, but underground networks of Protestant sympathizers continued to grow, especially among the lower aristocracy and some urban merchants who resented heavy church taxes and favored trade links with Protestant England.

---

4. The Rough Wooing and the Growth of Protestant Sympathy

James V died in 1542, leaving an infant daughter, Mary, Queen of Scots. As had happened before, Scotland faced another minority, which sparked power struggles among nobles. The English king, Henry VIII, tried to secure a marriage between young Mary, Queen of Scots, and his son Edward (the future Edward VI). This push, known as the "Rough Wooing," involved military invasions to force Scottish agreement. Notable events included the burning of Edinburgh in 1544 and the destructive campaign in the Borders. Many Scots, even Catholic-leaning lords, resented these violent tactics.

Counterintuitively, Henry VIII's aggression pushed some nobles to align with Catholic France for protection. Yet it also ignited anti-clerical feelings among others who believed the existing church hierarchy was failing to protect the country's interests. The French regent, Mary of Guise (mother of Mary, Queen of Scots), maintained a pro-Catholic stance but struggled to control a faction of Protestant lords—later known as the "Lords of the Congregation"—who viewed Protestantism as both a spiritual cause and a political opportunity to curb French domination.

Key developments during this period (1540s–1550s):

- **John Knox's Exile and Return**: Knox, initially a bodyguard to George Wishart, was captured by French forces in 1547 and served

as a galley slave. Released in 1549, he spent time in England and Geneva, absorbing Calvinist ideas. By the mid-1550s, Knox's writings, calling for a purified church and the overthrow of idolatry, circulated among Scottish lairds.
- **Emergence of the Lords of the Congregation**: Noble families like the Earls of Argyll, Glencairn, and Morton embraced Protestant ideas. They formed coalitions to resist the regent, Mary of Guise, demanding religious reform and an end to French interference.

As Mary, Queen of Scots, grew up in France (where she was betrothed to the Dauphin), the tension in Scotland escalated. Protestant-minded nobles saw an opening to reorganize the nation's church, especially if they could remove Catholic regents and sever ties with Catholic France.

---

5. The Reformation Crisis: 1557–1560

The critical turning point came between 1557 and 1560, a period of open conflict known as the Scottish Reformation Crisis. Several factors accelerated events:

1. **Lords of the Congregation's Formal Covenants**
   - In 1557, a group of Protestant nobles signed the "First Band," pledging mutual support for religious reform. Calling themselves the "Congregation," they aligned their movement with the broader European Reformation, encouraging local preaching and challenging Catholic rites.
2. **Mary of Guise's Hardline Measures**
   - The queen regent attempted to suppress Protestant assemblies, fueling resentment. She relied increasingly on French troops to maintain control, deepening suspicion that Scotland was being dragged into France's orbit.
3. **John Knox's Fiery Return (1559)**
   - Escaping from exile on the Continent, Knox returned to Scotland and began preaching vehemently against the Mass and Catholic imagery. Large crowds flocked to hear him. Knox's sermons in places like Perth triggered iconoclastic riots, with mobs destroying church statues and altars, acts the Protestant leaders often justified as purging "idolatry."

- The regent denounced these uprisings, labeling them rebellion. Knox's response was that Scripture authorized overthrowing ungodly rulers, a radical stance at the time.
4. **English Intervention**
    - Elizabeth I now reigned in England (from 1558), establishing a Protestant state. She faced the Catholic threat from France, especially as Mary, Queen of Scots (married to the French Dauphin), claimed a potential right to the English throne. To counter French influence in Scotland, Elizabeth's advisors supported the Lords of the Congregation with funds and, eventually, military aid.

By 1560, Mary of Guise was gravely ill and died in June that year. French troops, besieged in Leith by Scottish Protestants and English allies, reached a settlement. The resulting **Treaty of Edinburgh** (1560) effectively ended French dominance in Scotland. In the same year, the Scottish Parliament met and passed laws abolishing papal authority and the Catholic Mass, ushering in a legal Protestant Reformation.

---

6. Parliament of 1560: Establishing a Protestant Kirk

The Parliament of August 1560 proved transformative. Though Mary, Queen of Scots, was still in France and technically the sovereign, the Protestant lords took advantage of her absence to rewrite Scotland's religious laws:

- **Abolition of Papal Jurisdiction**: The Pope's authority in Scotland was declared null. All Catholic services—particularly the celebration of the Mass—were forbidden by statute.
- **Confession of Faith**: Parliament adopted the Scots Confession, largely drafted by John Knox and other ministers. Influenced by Calvinist doctrines, it emphasized the authority of Scripture, justification by faith, and the idea that a true church should be governed by elders (presbyters), not by bishops with territorial power.
- **Reorganization of Church Properties**: Although the intention was to redirect the wealth of abbeys and bishoprics to support the new Kirk and to fund education, much of that wealth ended up in noble

hands. This created friction, as the Protestant ministers found themselves under-resourced while nobles took advantage of monastic lands.

Despite these sweeping measures, the Reformation was not fully secure. Many parish priests and laypeople still held Catholic beliefs, especially in the Highlands and some Lowland pockets. Implementation of the new doctrines varied by region, and the new Kirk lacked the robust administrative structures that the old Catholic Church had painstakingly built over centuries. Moreover, Mary, Queen of Scots—who was Catholic—was about to return from France, adding fresh uncertainty.

---

7. Mary, Queen of Scots: A Catholic Monarch in a Protestant Country

In 1561, Mary returned to Scotland, newly widowed after the death of her husband, Francis II of France. At just 18, she was well-educated, fluent in French, and devoutly Catholic—yet she faced a Protestant establishment that had seized control in her absence. Key issues marked Mary's reign:

1. **Toleration vs. Distrust**:
    - Mary accepted that Scotland was now officially Protestant. She refrained from attempting to restore Catholicism en masse, perhaps recognizing the strength of Protestant nobles. However, she continued her personal Catholic worship, causing suspicion. Many Protestants, led by John Knox, viewed any Catholic practice as a dangerous step backward.
2. **Marriage Politics**:
    - Mary's marital decisions carried huge political ramifications. Her union with Lord Darnley (an English noble with claims to both English and Scottish thrones) in 1565 alienated key Protestant lords who feared a strengthening of Catholic influences. The marriage was tumultuous: Darnley was implicated in the murder of Mary's trusted secretary, David Rizzio, in 1566.
3. **Murder of Darnley and the Bothwell Affair (1567)**:

- Darnley's suspicious killing in 1567 outraged many nobles. Mary's subsequent marriage to the main suspect, James Hepburn, Earl of Bothwell, fueled rumors that she condoned or even orchestrated Darnley's murder. Protestant lords rose against her in rebellion.
- Forced to abdicate, Mary was imprisoned at Loch Leven Castle. Her infant son, James VI, was crowned King of Scots. Mary eventually escaped captivity in 1568, fleeing to England, where Elizabeth I kept her under house arrest for nearly 19 years before her execution in 1587.

Mary's downfall left the infant James VI to rule under regent governments—most of which were staunchly Protestant. This consolidated the Reformation's hold on Scotland, although royal politics remained fraught with competing factions. Meanwhile, John Knox continued preaching in Edinburgh until his death in 1572, providing ideological backbone to the Protestant Kirk.

---

8. The Kirk's Development Under Regent Governments

From 1567 to the early 1570s, Scotland was governed by a series of regents for the child-king James VI. Regents such as James Stewart, Earl of Moray, and Matthew Stewart, Earl of Lennox (both relatives of the royal family), struggled to stabilize the country:

- **Enforcement of the Reformation**
    - They worked to root out remaining Catholic strongholds, especially in the north and the Highlands, where some clans remained loyal to Mary or to older religious traditions.
    - Parliament passed acts reinforcing the prohibition of the Mass, and local leaders were encouraged to dismantle Catholic chapels. Still, the Kirk faced shortfalls in educated ministers and resources to staff every parish effectively.
- **Conflict with Mary's Allies**
    - A faction known as the "Queen's Party" or "Queen's Men" continued to support Mary's claim, leading to civil strife. Cities like Edinburgh and regions like the Borders could see shifting allegiances.

- o The regents often had to fight pitched battles against Mary's supporters. Regent Moray was assassinated in 1570, underscoring the danger of these power struggles.
- **Growing Presbyterian Structures**
  - o As time passed, the Kirk developed Presbyterian church courts (Sessions, Presbyteries, Synods, and the General Assembly) to manage doctrine and discipline. John Knox and other ministers argued that these assemblies, rather than bishops, should oversee spiritual matters.
  - o In 1572, some nobles tried to reinstall a form of episcopacy (appointing bishops) to maintain a hierarchical church. This "Tulchan" episcopacy was unpopular among strict Calvinists who saw bishops as remnants of Catholic corruption. The debate between Presbyterianism and limited episcopacy would simmer for decades.

Despite the turmoil, the Reformation's institutional foundation solidified. Protestant sermons and the reading of Scripture in the vernacular became more common. Literacy rates gradually improved as local communities established "reformed" schools, though progress was uneven. By the late 1570s, James VI's government had curtailed open Catholic worship, effectively marginalizing the old faith except in remote areas or at certain noble estates.

---

9. James VI Comes of Age: The King and the Kirk

Assuming personal rule in the early 1580s, James VI (by then a teenager) sought to balance the Kirk's influence with his own vision of royal authority:

- **Royal Supremacy vs. Presbyterian Ideals**:
  - o Influenced by theories of divine right monarchy, James VI believed that kings derived power from God directly, not from assemblies. By contrast, staunch Presbyterians viewed the church as governed by Christ alone, mediated through elders and assemblies, rather than by a single monarch or bishops.

- - James alternately placated and suppressed radical ministers who challenged his authority, such as Andrew Melville, a leading Presbyterian. Melville famously called James "God's silly vassal" to emphasize that the king was under God's law.
- **Anti-Catholic Laws**
  - James VI continued to enforce statutes against Catholic practices. However, he sometimes played a diplomatic game, especially if he considered a marriage alliance or sought political ties that might require some leniency toward Catholics.
  - A small Catholic minority persisted, often covertly, sometimes supported by powerful families who had private chapels. This minority presence would remain a point of tension, especially if European powers (like Spain or France) attempted to influence Scottish politics.
- **Cultural Flowering**
  - Under James VI, Scotland saw a minor cultural renaissance. The king himself was a writer, penning works such as "Basilikon Doron" (a treatise on kingship) and "Daemonologie" (on witchcraft). The court sponsored poets and scholars, furthering the development of Scots language literature.
  - Despite these cultural achievements, religious disputes did not abate. Ministers demanded freedom from royal interference, while James insisted on directing church appointments. Scotland's Reformation remained entangled with monarchical ambitions.

By 1603, an event would occur that changed the nature of Scotland's monarchy: James VI inherited the throne of England, becoming James I of England and Ireland as well. This "Union of the Crowns" profoundly altered Scotland's political and religious life, paving the way for further contention between the king's authority and the Kirk's desire for autonomy—matters we explore in the next chapter.

10. Social Impact of the Reformation

While high-level politics seized the headlines, the Reformation also touched everyday life across Scotland:

1. **Language and Worship**
   - Sermons and prayers in Scots or English replaced Latin liturgy, increasing lay participation and literacy. The printing of Bibles and catechisms in vernacular languages allowed more people to engage with Scripture directly.
2. **Moral Discipline**
   - Kirk sessions, the local church courts, oversaw moral behavior in communities. They imposed penalties for fornication, drunkenness, and Sabbath-breaking, among other offenses. Some found these measures intrusive, but others felt they promoted communal order.
3. **Education**
   - Protestant leaders championed the idea that everyone should read the Bible. Over time, they pressed for parish schools, though progress was uneven. Urban areas or Lowland parishes often developed basic schooling; remote rural communities lagged.
   - Universities like St. Andrews, Glasgow, and Aberdeen gradually reformed their curricula to include Protestant theology and broader humanist learning.
4. **Charity and Welfare**
   - The decline of monastic orders disrupted some traditional charitable functions, such as hospitality for travelers and aid to the poor. The new Kirk sometimes attempted to fill the gap, but resources were limited, and local parishes bore much of the burden.
5. **Violence and Confiscations**
   - The destruction of church ornaments and shrines—iconoclasm—remained controversial. For many devout Catholics, these actions were shocking desecrations. The seizure of church lands by noble patrons also created winners (nobles and some ministers) and losers (monks, friars, and devout laity).

- - Traditional festivals tied to saints' days were suppressed in some regions, replaced by simpler forms of worship. This cultural shift caused friction, as people lost communal traditions that had existed for centuries.

Over a single generation, Scotland transformed from a Catholic realm with strong French ties into a predominantly Protestant kingdom leaning toward Protestant England. This shift reshaped social norms, governance, and culture in ways still visible in the centuries that followed.

---

11. Conclusion

The Scottish Reformation was far more than a spiritual event. It intertwined with dynastic struggles, foreign alliances, and noble rivalries to produce a sweeping revolution in religious practice and national identity. Figures like John Knox preached a robust Calvinism that many Scots embraced, especially as it resonated with growing anti-French, anti-clerical sentiment. Parliamentary acts in 1560 dismantled the old Catholic hierarchy, replacing it with a Kirk that evolved Presbyterian structures distinct from the Anglican Church in England.

Mary, Queen of Scots, tried to balance her Catholic faith with the new Protestant settlement but failed amid scandal, rebellion, and her forced abdication. The regency governments that followed cemented the Reformation's gains. James VI (and later I of England) oversaw a Kirk that, though sometimes fractious, took root as a defining feature of Scottish society. By the turn of the 17th century, Scotland was firmly Protestant, albeit with lingering tensions between the crown's authority and the Kirk's demands for spiritual independence.

Now, as the next chapter will show, the momentous year of 1603 brought James VI to the English throne, inaugurating a "Union of the Crowns." This development would trigger new political and religious dynamics. Conflicts between royal power and Presbyterian zeal, between different noble factions, and between Scottish and English interests would only intensify. The Reformation had drastically changed the face of Scottish religion; the Union of the Crowns would change the shape of its monarchy and further test the country's unity.

CHAPTER 14

THE UNION OF THE CROWNS

1. Introduction

By the late 16th century, Scotland's monarchy, shaped by centuries of internal struggles and recently transformed by the Reformation, faced another dramatic change: the prospect that James VI would inherit the English throne. Since 1558, England had been ruled by Elizabeth I, the final monarch of the Tudor line. She remained unmarried and childless, which made her cousin James VI—himself the great-grandson of Margaret Tudor (Henry VIII's sister)—the leading candidate for succession. In 1603, Elizabeth died, and James VI duly became James I of England and Ireland, uniting the Scottish and English crowns under a single monarch for the first time.

This moment, known as the "Union of the Crowns," did not merge the two kingdoms into one state—at least not yet. Scotland and England remained separate political entities, each with its own parliament, laws, and church. However, they now shared a single ruler who spent most of his time in London rather than Edinburgh. This chapter explores the background of the Union of the Crowns, the consequences for Scottish governance and identity, and the early 17th-century developments that laid the groundwork for future conflicts involving the Stewart (Stuart) monarchs.

---

2. The Road to James VI's English Succession

Since the mid-1540s, English royalty had considered the possibility of uniting the kingdoms through marriage or direct inheritance. The "Rough Wooing" under Henry VIII had tried—and failed—to betroth Mary, Queen of Scots, to Prince Edward. That approach collapsed, but the Tudor and Stewart lines remained interconnected through James V's marriage to Mary of Guise and earlier links with Margaret Tudor (Henry VIII's elder sister). Elizabeth I's long reign (1558–1603), childless by choice and politically precarious at times, left the door open for James VI to become her successor.

Several factors smoothed James VI's path:

1. **Diplomatic Maneuvers**
    - Over the 1580s and 1590s, James VI carefully avoided alienating Elizabeth. He discouraged direct French involvement in Scotland, curbed radical Catholic activities, and even extradited some dissidents. By showing himself as a stable Protestant king, James won favor among influential English courtiers who had no wish to see a Catholic claimant on the English throne (like Spain's Infanta or Mary, Queen of Scots).
2. **Execution of Mary, Queen of Scots**
    - Elizabeth I ultimately executed Mary, Queen of Scots, in 1587, accusing her of involvement in plots against the English crown. Although Mary's death could have strained Scottish-English relations, James VI pragmatically kept diplomatic ties. He recognized that protesting his mother's execution too fiercely might harm his inheritance prospects.
3. **English Noble Support**
    - Many English lords, exhausted by religious strife and eager to avoid a disputed succession, accepted James VI's claim, seeing him as the nearest legitimate Protestant heir. Elizabeth I's own council advised her to make no official declaration but tacitly prepared for James's accession.

When Elizabeth died in March 1603, James VI rode south to London, hailed by many English subjects who hoped he would unify the realms in peace and Protestant faith. Thus began the Stewart monarchy's rule over both Scotland and England. James styled himself "King of Great Britain, France, and Ireland," though no formal legislative union existed yet.

3. Initial Effects on Scotland: Absentee Monarchy and Governance

The Union of the Crowns meant that the king—once physically present at the Scottish court—now resided primarily in England. This absence drastically changed Scottish governance:

- **Royal Court Moves South**
    - James VI/I relocated to London, bringing along some Scottish courtiers but mostly immersed himself in the wealthier, more populous realm of England. Scotland's noble class found fewer opportunities to influence the king face-to-face. Ambitious Scots had to travel to London if they wanted royal patronage, often leaving behind local obligations.
- **Scottish Privy Council and Parliament**
    - In James's absence, the Scottish Privy Council and Parliament handled day-to-day affairs. The Privy Council, composed of influential nobles and church figures, effectively managed internal security, justice, and financial matters. While James occasionally summoned the Scottish Parliament, sessions became less frequent.
    - The crown still appointed key officeholders in Scotland—like the Chancellor, the Treasurer, or the Secretary—but these figures might serve the king's interests from afar, occasionally overshadowing local concerns.
- **Local Oligarchies and Clan Chiefs**
    - With the royal presence diminished, powerful lords or clan chiefs in the Highlands, Borders, and Isles acted more autonomously. Some took advantage of the reduced direct oversight to press local claims, engage in feuds, or strengthen personal followings.
    - James tried to impose new policies (e.g., pacification of the Borders by dismantling reiving clans, or "civilizing" Highland chiefs), but enforcement was inconsistent without the king's physical presence.
- **Economic Consequences**
    - Scotland did not immediately gain large economic benefits from the personal union. Tariffs, trade laws, and separate

parliaments remained in place. English merchants often held a competitive edge in broader markets, leaving Scots to negotiate from a weaker position.
- Nevertheless, some Scots enjoyed careers at the English court or found new markets for Scottish goods, forging personal or commercial links in London.

In sum, while James's dual kingship elevated Scotland's monarch to a grander stage, it also left the kingdom somewhat neglected in daily governance, fueling noble jockeying for power and resentment at the lack of direct royal attention.

---

4. Religious Implications: Balancing Anglicanism and the Scottish Kirk

As King of England, James inherited the Church of England's episcopal structure, which had bishops and a hierarchical form similar to Catholicism but recognized the monarch as supreme governor rather than the Pope. Meanwhile, Scotland's Reformed Kirk, heavily influenced by Presbyterian ideals, distrusted bishops and embraced local church governance through elders and assemblies.

James believed in a form of episcopacy, liking the idea that bishops could help him control the church. He famously quipped, "No bishop, no king," implying that a strictly Presbyterian system undermined monarchical authority. After 1603, he pursued the following strategies:

1. **Attempted Restoration of Scottish Bishops**
    - James appointed or revived bishoprics in Scotland, empowering certain ministers (sometimes called "Tulchan bishops" earlier on) to oversee dioceses. He insisted that these bishops still be aligned with Reformed doctrine, hoping for a middle ground that would satisfy some Scots without adopting full Presbyterian governance.
2. **Five Articles of Perth (1618)**
    - In 1618, James pushed through the Five Articles of Perth at a General Assembly, mandating practices like kneeling at

communion, private baptism, and confirmation by bishops. Many Presbyterian ministers saw these articles as creeping Anglican ritual, not supported by Scripture.
    - Although initially enforced with limited success, the articles fueled deeper resentment, setting the stage for future conflicts under James's son, Charles I.
  3. **Tolerance for Catholics?**
     - Officially, James remained anti-Catholic, especially after the Gunpowder Plot of 1605 in England, where Catholic conspirators aimed to blow up the king and parliament. Yet James also tried to maintain diplomatic ties with Catholic powers like Spain, sometimes easing persecution of Scottish Catholics if it served diplomatic ends.
     - Strict Protestants in Scotland regarded any tolerance toward Catholics as a betrayal of the Reformation.

By the time of James's death in 1625, the Kirk was uneasy but not yet in open revolt. His balancing act had partially restored a moderate episcopacy in Scotland, yet many ministers privately (or openly) opposed it. Once Charles I ascended, his harsher approach to imposing religious uniformity would spark crises that dwarfed James's challenges.

---

5. Political Maneuvering and Noble Discontent

While James VI was a seasoned political operator—adept at playing factions against each other—his long absences allowed certain noble families to dominate the Scottish court. Among the notable developments:

- **Privy Council Dominance**
  - High-level officers (like the Chancellor, Earl of Dunfermline, or the Secretary, Earl of Dunbar, etc.) wielded considerable sway. They managed patronage—grants of titles, lands, or pensions—creating networks of support or rivalry.
  - Local power-brokers often aligned with or opposed these central figures, leading to shifting alliances. Some nobles resented the "king's favorites" who benefited from direct access in London.

- **Clan Consolidation**
    - James oversaw efforts to tame the Borders (formerly known for clan feuds and raids). Known reiving families faced the "Pacification of the Borders," involving harsh punishments, demolitions of fortified houses, and forced relocation. A measure of success reduced large-scale raiding by the 1620s.
    - In the Highlands, attempts to neutralize the MacGregors and bring the MacDonalds under tighter control were partly successful, though clan law continued. Private feuds—like the Glen Coe area disputes or expansions by the Campbells—carried on with limited royal supervision.
- **Burghs and Merchants**
    - Urban centers grew in importance, especially Edinburgh, Aberdeen, and Glasgow. Merchants there sought charters from the crown, fostering trade with the Low Countries or the Baltic region. Without consistent royal attention, tensions sometimes arose between noble landholders and rising urban guilds.
    - Some burghs welcomed James's personal union if it opened new English markets for Scottish goods (like salted fish, wool, hides), though the actual gains were modest due to separate economic policies in each kingdom.

While the monarchy maintained broad control, the complex interplay of royal absenteeism, local aristocratic power, and burgh ambitions set the stage for further friction once the more dogmatic Charles I took the throne.

---

6. Cultural and Intellectual Effects of the Union

Despite the administrative challenges, the Union of the Crowns did foster a certain cultural interchange:

1. **Movement of People**
    - Scottish courtiers, scholars, and merchants traveled to London, bringing new influences home. Conversely, some

English gentry visited Scotland, though less frequently, given London's allure for political and cultural life.
    - Noble families sometimes educated their children at English universities or engaged tutors who were conversant in English high culture. This cross-border flow contributed to shifts in taste for architecture, dress, and courtly manners.
2. **Literature and Language**
    - The Scots language (a close cousin to northern English dialects) encountered the growing prestige of standardizing English from London's court. Over time, some upper-class Scots increasingly wrote in an English style to improve opportunities at the southern court.
    - Poets and dramatists in Scotland found fewer royal patrons at home, resulting in a partial decline of distinctly Scots-language literary output at the highest levels. Nonetheless, popular ballads and folk traditions flourished in the countryside.
3. **Religion and Scholarship**
    - Some Scottish ministers visited England's universities, exchanging ideas with Anglican theologians or encountering Puritan teachings. This broad exposure influenced debates within the Kirk, fueling both moderate and more radical perspectives.
    - King James himself supported biblical scholarship, famously commissioning the "Authorized" or "King James" version of the Bible (1611) in England. Although intended primarily for the English Church, it eventually circulated widely in Scotland, shaping religious language among literate believers.

Thus, the personal union expanded horizons for certain elites but also began a slow process where many Scots oriented themselves toward English standards to gain favor or career advancement. Meanwhile, local traditions persisted, especially in more remote regions or within Gaelic-speaking communities, less touched by the royal court's transformations.

7. James VI/I's Legacy in Scotland

James died in 1625, leaving behind a complex legacy for Scotland:

- **Stability vs. Tension**
    - On one hand, his reign completed the Reformation's entrenchment and suppressed major internal revolts, achieving relative stability. On the other, his preference for episcopacy sowed seeds of conflict with strict Presbyterians, who believed the Kirk was heading back toward "popish" ceremonies.
- **Weaker Parliamentary Traditions?**
    - James's long absences meant fewer regular Scottish parliamentary sessions, reducing the habit of collaborative legislation. Some argue this weakened the kingdom's parliamentary culture, making future kings more prone to govern by decree or through select advisors.
- **Frustration of the Nobles**
    - Many lords found it harder to compete for royal influence without traveling to London. They sometimes felt overshadowed by English peers or by a handful of Scots with special access to James, creating simmering resentments.
- **Foundation for Later Conflicts**
    - The seeds of the 17th-century religious wars in Scotland had been planted. A more immediate confrontation over liturgical reforms and the role of bishops would erupt under Charles I, culminating in the 1637 Prayer Book crisis and the Covenanters' rebellion—topics to be explored in later chapters.

In sum, James's personal union signaled the dawn of a new era in which Scotland shared a monarch with England. While no formal legislative union existed, the monarchy's center of gravity decisively shifted south. This reorientation carried both opportunities (broader cultural contacts, avoidance of another English-Scottish war) and drawbacks (less direct monarchy, uncertain assimilation of religious practices). Soon, these tensions would boil over, testing the fragile bonds between crown, Kirk, and nobles.

8. The Road Toward a Fuller Union (and Future Conflicts)

The Union of the Crowns did not immediately unify Scotland and England in law or government. Each kingdom retained its own parliament, church, and legal system. Nonetheless, James VI/I—referring to himself as "King of Great Britain"—yearned for a complete union. He pushed for a single parliament, uniform trade rules, and consistent religion across his domains. English and Scottish parliaments resisted, unwilling to surrender local privileges.

Over the next decades, the monarchy's attempts to impose religious uniformity and new forms of governance triggered deep unrest, especially under Charles I. The ripple effects included:

- **Covenanter Movement**
    - Outraged by Charles I's imposition of an Anglican-style prayer book in 1637, Scottish Presbyterians signed the National Covenant to defend their Kirk's freedoms. This set off the Bishops' Wars (1639–1640), effectively challenging royal authority and renewing old questions about whether Scotland could be forced into English-style worship.
- **Civil Wars in All Three Kingdoms**
    - As friction deepened in England too—leading to the English Civil War (1642–1651)—Scotland's role became entangled with that conflict. Alliances and counter-alliances formed, culminating in the Covenanters playing a major part in the downfall of Charles I.
    - Though these events belong to later chapters, it is clear that the personal union introduced under James VI/I was the foundation upon which the eventual "Wars of the Three Kingdoms" were built.

Thus, the seeds sown in 1603 would yield a harvest of both closer ties and painful divisions. Scotland maintained its distinct institutions yet was never again free from the gravitational pull of England's much larger population, economy, and political stage.

9. Conclusion

The Union of the Crowns in 1603 stands as a watershed in Scottish history, bringing King James VI north of the Tweed onto the English throne as James I. For Scotland, this meant an absentee monarchy that complicated governance, an emerging tension between Presbyterian Calvinism and episcopal authority, and a slow shift of cultural and economic influence toward London. Meanwhile, James's skillful diplomacy kept large-scale conflicts at bay during his lifetime, preserving a measure of stability.

Yet not all was resolved. The immediate lack of a formal legislative union meant that Scotland and England each continued with separate parliaments and laws, a situation that left open the question of how these two realms should coexist under a single crown. Religious disputes—particularly over bishoprics and liturgical practices—festered, setting the stage for the Covenanter movement under Charles I. Before long, the Stuarts would find themselves embroiled in civil wars that would shake the entire British Isles.

For now, we close the story at the dawn of the 17th century, with Scotland newly reoriented by James VI's personal union. The next chapters will cover how these seeds of tension and evolving alliances played out, leading to the Covenanters, civil wars, and profound changes in the monarchy's role—both in Scotland and across the British Isles.

CHAPTER 15

THE COVENANTERS AND CIVIL WAR

1. Introduction

By the early 17th century, Scotland had undergone a Reformation that established a predominantly Calvinist Church (the Kirk). However, tensions over church governance persisted. James VI (also James I of England), believing "No bishop, no king," favored a moderate episcopacy in Scotland. Many ministers, influenced by Presbyterian ideals, resented such top-down structures. When Charles I ascended the thrones of Scotland, England, and Ireland in 1625, he further pressed his vision of a uniform church across his three kingdoms—one that included bishops and liturgical practices that strict Presbyterians saw as dangerously close to Catholicism.

These conflicts erupted in 1637 when Charles tried to impose a new prayer book on the Scottish Kirk. Indignant, many Scots believed the king was trampling upon their Reformed faith. Riots, petitions, and eventually formal covenants emerged to reject royal religious policies. Thus began the era of the Covenanters—Protestants who pledged to defend Scotland's Presbyterian traditions. Their stance against royal edicts led to multiple armed confrontations, known collectively as the Bishops' Wars, and eventually intertwined with civil conflicts in England and Ireland, culminating in the Wars of the Three Kingdoms. This chapter examines the roots of the Covenanting movement, the major flashpoints of war, the shifting alliances, and how these tumultuous events reshaped Scotland's politics and religious identity.

---

2. Seeds of Discontent Under Charles I

Charles I inherited his father's preference for episcopacy but lacked James VI/I's political finesse. Key steps that fueled discontent:

- **Arminian Influence and Laudian Reforms**

- Charles embraced the theology of William Laud, Archbishop of Canterbury in England. Laud's "Arminian" leanings and emphasis on ritual offended strict Calvinists who championed predestination and plain worship. Laud encouraged altars, liturgical ceremonies, and hierarchical vestments—a stark contrast to the simpler Presbyterian style in Scotland.
- **Revived Scottish Bishoprics**
    - Building on James's partial restoration, Charles bolstered the role of Scottish bishops, granting them political authority and seats on the Scottish Privy Council. Many ministers who held Presbyterian convictions felt sidelined or bullied by these episcopal superiors.
- **Act of Revocation (1625)**
    - Early in his reign, Charles attempted to revoke certain land grants, including former Church lands that nobles had acquired since the Reformation. Although the king later negotiated some exemptions, his initial move alarmed the aristocracy, who feared losing property and privileges. Resentments festered, bridging some noble interests with the Presbyterian cause.
- **Lack of a Scottish Coronation Parliament**
    - Although Charles visited Scotland in 1633 for a coronation ceremony at Holyrood, he convened only a short Parliament that rubber-stamped his reforms. He took little time to listen to local concerns, alienating many. Also, the coronation included elaborate Anglican-style rites in St Giles' Cathedral, unsettling Scots who saw "Romish" pomp in these ceremonies.

Throughout the 1630s, Charles governed Scotland primarily through bishops and a handful of advisors. This top-down approach kept many leading nobles, ministers, and burgh representatives away from policy-making, building quiet resentment that would soon boil over with the prayer book crisis.

3. The 1637 Prayer Book Crisis and Public Outrage

The tipping point arrived when Charles I and Archbishop Laud introduced a new liturgy for the Scottish Church, commonly called the "Laudian Prayer Book." Though nominally akin to the English Book of Common Prayer, it had additional ceremonial elements that alarmed many Scots. The king mandated its use from July 1637 onward.

- **Riot at St Giles' Cathedral**
    - On 23 July 1637, Edinburgh's St Giles' Cathedral saw open disruption. When the dean began reading from the new prayer book, a crowd erupted in protest. Tradition (possibly apocryphal) credits Jenny Geddes—a market-trader woman—for throwing a stool at the officiating minister, shouting, "Dost thou say Mass in my lug?" The scene turned chaotic, setting a precedent for further resistance.
- **Spread of Resistance**
    - Protests erupted across Lowland parishes, with some congregations refusing to let clergy read from the prayer book. Royal officials tried to enforce compliance, but local magistrates often sided with the protesters. In towns like Glasgow, Perth, and Dundee, sessions and burgh councils denounced the liturgy as unscriptural and "popish."
- **Petitions and Tables**
    - Leading noblemen, ministers, and burgesses formed "Tables," ad hoc committees to coordinate opposition. They gathered petitions demanding withdrawal of the new liturgy. As the crown refused to concede, the opposition hardened.

Charles misjudged the depth of the backlash. He believed a firm stance would quell rebellion, but in reality, the movement escalated, culminating in a national covenant that would unite various groups under a common pledge to defend Presbyterianism.

4. The National Covenant (1638): Birth of the Covenanters

Seeing no relief from royal decrees, Scottish Protestants turned to a collective covenant, drawing on a tradition that extended back to earlier "bands" and confessions. John Knox had once advised using covenants to unify believers; now, the strategy returned with new vigor.

- **Drafting the Covenant**
    - Ministers and lay leaders combined prior documents—such as the Scots Confession of 1560 and earlier pledges to reject "popish" doctrines—into a comprehensive agreement that also disavowed any future acts contrary to Reformed faith. They reaffirmed loyalty to the king in civil matters but insisted on the independence of the Kirk in spiritual affairs.
- **Signing in Greyfriars Kirkyard**
    - On 28 February 1638, a large crowd gathered in the kirkyard of Greyfriars Church, Edinburgh, to sign the National Covenant. Noblemen, ministers, merchants, and commoners lined up to place their names (or marks) on the document. Some pricked their arms to sign in blood, symbolizing fervent commitment.
- **Widespread Adoption**
    - Word spread across the Lowlands and parts of the Highlands, with congregations queueing to sign. Elders read the Covenant aloud in parish after parish. Although a minority dissented—some bishops, certain royalist nobles—most Presbyterian-minded Scots embraced it as a holy duty.

The Covenanters believed they were defending Scotland's Reformation heritage against royal innovations. Despite pledges of loyalty to Charles, their actions effectively repudiated his ecclesiastical authority. In late 1638, a Glasgow General Assembly abolished bishops altogether, returning the Kirk to full Presbyterian governance. This direct challenge to the crown's prerogatives made conflict inevitable.

5. The Bishops' Wars (1639–1640)

Charles I responded by assembling forces to subdue the rebellious Scots, launching a pair of conflicts known as the Bishops' Wars. However, the king's lack of funds and the rising discontent in England hobbled his campaigns:

First Bishops' War (1639)

- **Scottish Preparations**
    - The Covenanters, aided by experienced soldiers who had fought in the Thirty Years' War on the Continent, rapidly organized an army. They appointed notable generals like Alexander Leslie, who fortified strongpoints and prepared to meet any royal incursion from England.
- **Pacification of Berwick**
    - Charles advanced to Berwick-upon-Tweed with an English force but discovered his troops poorly trained and reluctant. Realizing a direct assault would be risky, the king negotiated a temporary truce in June 1639, known as the Pacification of Berwick. Both sides agreed to disband armies and hold a free Scottish General Assembly.
    - Despite the official ceasefire, fundamental issues remained unresolved.

Second Bishops' War (1640)

- **English Frustrations**
    - Charles reconvened the English Parliament in spring 1640 to request funds, but the so-called "Short Parliament" refused to grant money for war against the Scots, demanding redress of grievances instead. Annoyed, Charles dissolved it after a few weeks, again lacking the resources to mount a robust offensive.
- **Covenanter Offensive**
    - The Scottish army marched into northern England late that summer, defeating a hastily raised English force at the Battle of Newburn near Newcastle. Occupying

Northumberland and Durham, the Covenanters demanded Charles pay for their costs of occupation.
- By October 1640, Charles—forced by financial and political desperation—agreed to the Treaty of Ripon, promising to pay the Scots a large daily sum until a final settlement. He had to recall the English Parliament in November (the "Long Parliament"), effectively ceding much authority to English MPs who resented his personal rule.

The Bishops' Wars ended with the Covenanters triumphant. They secured major concessions for the Presbyterian Kirk in Scotland and gained influence over English politics by occupying the north. Meanwhile, Charles's difficulties in raising money and controlling Parliament ignited a similar crisis in England, leading toward civil war there. Scotland's Covenanter movement thus became a key factor in the broader Wars of the Three Kingdoms.

---

6. Scotland in the Wider Wars of the Three Kingdoms (1642–1649)

After 1640, England spiraled into civil war between Charles I and parliamentary forces. Scotland's Covenanters, flush from victory, faced new dilemmas:

- **Solemn League and Covenant (1643)**
    - Seeing an opportunity to secure Presbyterianism across Britain, Scottish leaders negotiated with the English Parliament. In 1643, both sides signed the Solemn League and Covenant, promising mutual defense of the "reformed religion" and—critically—committing England to a Presbyterian church settlement if Parliament prevailed over the king.
    - Many in the English Parliament agreed only to gain Scotland's military help, but they remained uneasy about imposing Presbyterianism on all of England.
- **Scottish Intervention in England**

- A Covenanter army crossed the border in January 1644 to fight alongside English Parliamentarians against Royalist forces. Early successes, such as the victory at Marston Moor (July 1644), showcased Scottish contribution. However, tensions arose when the English "Independent" faction gained ground, resisting a strict Presbyterian settlement.
- **Montrose's Royalist Campaign in Scotland**
    - Meanwhile, James Graham, Marquis of Montrose, led a Royalist uprising in Scotland (1644-1645). Backed by some Highland clans (particularly MacDonalds) and Irish Confederates, Montrose's small yet mobile force won several battles—e.g., Tippermuir, Inverlochy—seemingly outmatching Covenanter armies.
    - Despite these striking victories, Montrose lacked strong Lowland support and eventually faced a larger Covenanter force. By late 1645, his campaign collapsed, reaffirming Covenanter control of Scotland.
- **King's Surrender and Execution**
    - In 1646, Charles I surrendered to the Scottish army near Newark, hoping for leniency. The Covenanters, suspecting the king would never concede Presbyterian demands, handed him over to the English Parliament in exchange for financial recompense.
    - After brief interludes of negotiation, Charles was tried and executed by the English Parliament in January 1649—an unprecedented regicide that horrified many Scots, even some Covenanters.

This phase ended with Covenanters again dominant in Scotland, but deeply uneasy about radical developments in England. The monarchy's collapse south of the border left the Scots uncertain about their own future governance, culminating in a brief alliance with Charles II—Charles I's son—in a last attempt to restore the Stewart line under Presbyterian terms.

---

7. The Rise and Fall of the Covenanter Regime

With Charles I's execution, the English Commonwealth under Oliver Cromwell emerged, abolishing the monarchy in England. Scotland's reaction was to proclaim Charles II king—on condition that he sign the Covenant and enforce Presbyterianism:

- **Coronation of Charles II at Scone (1651)**
    - Despite reservations about Charles II's genuine commitment to the Covenant, Scots crowned him at Scone in January 1651, hoping he would champion Presbyterian unity against Cromwell's republican regime. But the relationship was uneasy: the Covenanting leadership demanded strict moral codes and sometimes excluded Royalist supporters from the new king's council.
- **Invasion by Cromwell**
    - Oliver Cromwell's New Model Army invaded Scotland in 1650, defeating a Covenanter force at Dunbar. The following year, Charles II led a desperate invasion of England from the north, culminating in the Battle of Worcester (1651), a catastrophic defeat. Charles fled to the Continent, leaving Scotland under English occupation.
- **English Occupation (1652–1660)**
    - Cromwell's Commonwealth annexed Scotland, dissolving the Scottish Parliament. A network of garrisons enforced order, while a variety of taxes funded the occupation. For many Scots, this period was humiliating, though some found that Cromwell's rule was administratively efficient and allowed religious toleration beyond strict Presbyterian lines.
    - Covenanter factions split into "Resolutioners," who believed in working with Charles II, and "Protesters," who insisted on a purer covenant free from political compromises. These schisms weakened the movement.

By the mid-1650s, Scottish national governance was effectively defunct, overshadowed by English republican rule. The Covenanters' dream of a fully Presbyterian Britain had shattered, undone by internal divisions, Montrose's Royalist revolt, and Cromwell's superior military. Yet the restoration of the monarchy loomed on the horizon, as Cromwell's Commonwealth faced internal strains after his death in 1658.

---

8. The Restoration and Aftermath for Covenanters (1660–1662)

In 1660, General George Monck led troops from Scotland into England to restore the monarchy. Charles II returned triumphantly to London, ushering in the Restoration:

- **Charles II's Policy Toward Scotland**
    - Initially, Scots hoped for a renewal of covenant ideals. But Charles II, scarred by his earlier experience, had no desire to be bound again by Presbyterian demands. Instead, he reestablished episcopacy in Scotland (1662), ignoring previous Covenanting settlements.
- **Repression of Covenanters**
    - The government persecuted ministers who refused episcopal authority, driving some into open defiance. New laws criminalized conventicles (unauthorized worship gatherings) and demanded strict loyalty oaths.
    - Many Covenanters fled to remote moorlands or held secret field meetings ("conventicles"), risking fines or imprisonment. The "Killing Time" of the 1680s would see heightened persecution under Charles II and his successor, James VII (James II of England).
- **Noble and Ministerial Divisions**
    - Some influential Presbyterians accepted a compromise or conformed outwardly to the restored episcopacy. Others, outraged, became radicalized, seeing the monarchy as apostate.
    - The once-powerful Covenanting coalition fragmented, losing the broad unity it had enjoyed in the 1640s.

Thus, by the early 1660s, the grand era of the Covenanters as a ruling force had ended. Their attempt to shape Scotland (and Britain) under strict Presbyterian lines collapsed under the Restoration monarchy's crackdown.

However, pockets of religious dissent continued, sowing seeds for future uprisings and controversies.

---

9. Lasting Consequences of the Covenanting Era

Though the Covenanter regime itself was short-lived, its imprint on Scotland was profound:

1. **Presbyterian Identity**
    - The Covenants legitimized a deep-rooted Presbyterian consciousness, emphasizing that the church must be free from state interference. Even after official institutions shifted, lay communities retained the memory of sworn covenants that upheld the pure Reformed gospel.
2. **Civil War Trauma**
    - Warfare from the Bishops' Wars to the final battles under Cromwell devastated parts of the Lowlands and Highlands. Farms were burned, families uprooted, and local economies disrupted by garrisons, foraging armies, and forced exactions. Scotland emerged economically weakened.
3. **Rise of Radical Sects**
    - The period of upheaval allowed more radical religious groups (some influenced by English Independents or even Quakers) to form small congregations, challenging the uniformity sought by the mainstream Kirk.
4. **Political Lessons**
    - Noble families discovered that controlling a rebellious Kirk and a mobilized laity was no simple task. The monarchy, for its part, learned that ignoring Scottish concerns could unleash powerful rebellions, forcing the crown to balance religious preferences with local sentiment.
5. **Legacy of Constitutional Ideas**
    - The Covenanters advanced arguments about lawful resistance to ungodly rulers, laying intellectual groundwork for later debates on the rights of subjects versus monarchs. Although overshadowed by events in England, these ideas would resurface in the Glorious Revolution and beyond.

Hence, the Covenanting era had forged a fiery brand of Presbyterian nationalism that would erupt time and again whenever the monarchy or bishops overstepped their bounds. While the immediate result was Restoration persecution, the stage was set for further showdowns that would shape Scottish and British history.

---

10. Conclusion

The mid-17th century found Scotland at the heart of a larger British crisis, with the Covenanter movement igniting conflict over church governance and the limits of royal power. The National Covenant (1638) and subsequent Bishops' Wars exposed Charles I's inability to impose a uniform liturgy on a determined populace. The Covenanters emerged as a potent force, seizing control of Scotland's government and influencing the English Civil War through the Solemn League and Covenant. Yet their triumph was short-lived. Internal splits, Montrose's Royalist insurrection, and Oliver Cromwell's invasion brought Scotland under English occupation. The Restoration of Charles II in 1660 further reversed Presbyterian gains, leading to renewed episcopacy and harsh suppression of dissent.

Although the Covenanter ascendancy waned, their legacy endured in Scotland's religious psyche, embedding the principle that a people could lawfully resist rulers who violated the church's autonomy. This tension between crown and Kirk would persist, fueling subsequent unrest and shaping political discourse. Next, we turn to Chapter 16 to see how the aftermath of the Restoration, the eventual Glorious Revolution, and the Jacobite cause played out, culminating in a new era of political transformations across the British Isles.

CHAPTER 16

THE GLORIOUS REVOLUTION AND THE JACOBITES

1. Introduction

After the turbulent mid-17th century—marked by the Civil Wars, Cromwellian occupation, and the Restoration—Scotland entered the reigns of Charles II (1660–1685) and his brother James VII (James II of England, 1685–1688). Both kings maintained an episcopal structure in the Scottish Church and persecuted radical Presbyterians (the so-called "Covenanting Remnant"), fueling ongoing resentment. However, the deeper fault line lay in James VII's open Catholic faith. Many Scots, still fiercely Protestant, regarded a Catholic monarch as a dire threat to the Reformation legacy. When James VII had a Catholic son in 1688, fears mounted of a permanent Catholic dynasty.

England's Glorious Revolution forced James VII from the throne, installing William of Orange and Mary (James's Protestant daughter) as co-monarchs. Scotland swiftly followed suit, deposing James and proclaiming William and Mary in 1689. Yet not all Scots accepted this outcome. Some highland clans, notably the MacDonalds, Camerons, and others with ties to the exiled Stewart line, rose in armed support of James. These "Jacobites" (from "Jacobus," Latin for James) would stage multiple rebellions into the mid-18th century. This chapter delves into how the Glorious Revolution played out in Scotland, the early Jacobite risings, the shifting alliances between crown and Kirk, and the broader transformations that led Scotland toward an eventual union of parliaments in 1707.

---

2. Religious Tensions Under Charles II and James VII

Following the Restoration in 1660, Charles II reimposed episcopacy on the Church of Scotland. Civil authorities harassed and punished those who defied bishop-led worship:

- **Dragoons and Field Preachings**

- - Charles II's government sent armed dragoons into Lowland areas to suppress illegal conventicles (outdoor worship services). Conventiclers believed they obeyed God rather than a worldly king who threatened Presbyterian purity.
  - Intermittent risings (like the Pentland Rising in 1666, the Bothwell Bridge rebellion in 1679) showed how pockets of militant Covenanters clung to the old National Covenant. The crown crushed these efforts, executing or banishing participants.
- **James, Duke of York, as Royal Commissioner**
  - Before becoming king, James (Duke of York) served in Scotland as his brother's representative. Openly Catholic, he escalated persecution of extreme Presbyterians. This "Killing Time" (1680s) saw figures like Richard Cameron or Donald Cargill martyred for refusing royal authority in religious matters.
- **James VII's Accession (1685)**
  - When Charles II died, James VII inherited the throne, confirming many Scots' worst fears of a Catholic monarch. He tried to ease penal laws against Catholics, hoping for toleration, but most Presbyterian Scots saw any Catholic privilege as an existential threat.

Thus, by the late 1680s, the stage was set for upheaval. James's Catholicism collided with Scottish Protestant convictions, fueling the desire for a regime change that aligned with Reformed principles. English concerns over James's Catholic male heir only heightened the crisis, leading to William of Orange's invitation to assume the English throne.

---

3. The Glorious Revolution Reaches Scotland (1688–1689)

When William of Orange landed in England (November 1688), James VII fled to France. The English Parliament declared the throne vacant, offering it to William and his wife Mary (James's Protestant daughter). Scottish events unfolded in parallel:

- **Convention of Estates (1689)**
    - In Scotland, a hastily summoned Convention of Estates met in Edinburgh to decide the monarchy's future. Strongly influenced by Presbyterian nobles and burgh representatives, the Convention adopted the "Claim of Right," proclaiming that James had forfeited the throne by violating Scottish laws and "subverting the Protestant religion."
    - They offered the crown to William and Mary, who accepted. In May 1689, the Scottish Convention formalized this settlement, effectively deposing James.
- **Religious Settlement**
    - William, seeking broad support, allowed Scotland to re-establish Presbyterian governance in the Kirk. The 1689 "Act Abolishing Prelacy" ended bishops' authority. A subsequent act in 1690 ratified Presbyterianism as the established Church of Scotland. This step fulfilled many Covenanters' aspirations, though it fell short of reinstating the original Covenant in full.
- **Jacobite Opposition**
    - Not all Scots accepted the new regime. Some Highland clans and staunch royalists upheld James's divine right as a Stewart king. Their frustration soon sparked armed revolt, an early Jacobite campaign led by figures like John Graham of Claverhouse ("Bonnie Dundee").

Thus, the Glorious Revolution in Scotland replaced an unpopular Catholic king with a Protestant monarchy that embraced Presbyterianism. Yet dividing lines between Jacobites and Williamites—often overlapping with clan loyalties—now shaped Scotland's political landscape, setting off a cycle of insurrections and government crackdowns.

---

4. The First Jacobite Rising (1689–1691)

Soon after William and Mary's accession, John Graham of Claverhouse, Viscount Dundee, rallied Highland clans loyal to James VII:

- **Battle of Killiecrankie (1689)**
    - Dundee's forces, largely Highlanders skilled in swift charges, routed a government army at Killiecrankie Pass in July 1689. The victory showcased the fearsome Highland "Highland Charge." However, Dundee himself died in battle, depriving the Jacobites of a unifying commander.
    - Without Dundee's leadership, subsequent engagements (such as at Dunkeld) went poorly for Jacobites, who lacked coordination and resources.
- **Jacobite Weakness**
    - Charles II and James VII never fully invested in building a robust base in the Highlands, leaving clan support fragmented. Many clan chiefs demanded significant subsidies or strategic assurance to commit to rebellion.
    - William's government, though still consolidating power, offered pardons or bribes to clan leaders, eroding Jacobite unity.
- **Glencoe Massacre (1692)**
    - The culminating atrocity was the Massacre of Glencoe in February 1692. Government troops, under the pretext that the MacDonald clan of Glencoe had missed a deadline to swear allegiance, killed at least 38 MacDonalds in their homes. The incident became symbolic of the Williamite government's harsh approach, though it ultimately stirred more resentment than it quelled.

By 1691, most Highland chiefs submitted to William's authority. The first major Jacobite rising petered out, leaving a legacy of bitterness among those clans who believed their loyalty to the Stewart line had been repaid with violence or neglect.

---

5. The Williamite Era and Economic Challenges

With the Jacobite threat temporarily contained, William's regime turned to governance. Scotland, however, faced significant economic hurdles:

- **Darien Scheme (1695–1700)**

- Scotland's Parliament chartered the "Company of Scotland" to establish a trading colony at Darien (on the Isthmus of Panama). Many Scots invested heavily, seeing it as a route to wealth and a gateway to overseas trade networks.
- The expedition failed disastrously due to disease, Spanish hostility, and lack of English support. Thousands died, and the financial ruin struck at all levels of Scottish society, creating resentment toward England, whose East India Company had undermined the venture.

- **Religious Settlements and Ongoing Dissent**
    - The 1690 Settlement made Presbyterianism the official church, but tensions persisted. Some Episcopalian communities, particularly in the northeast, felt alienated. The new Presbyterian Kirk also faced internal splits over how strictly it should adhere to old Covenanting principles.
    - William's "Revolution Church" was moderate, allowing a broad range of Calvinist opinion but refusing to readmit bishops or extreme Covenanter demands. This compromise disappointed hardcore Presbyterians and angered staunch royalists.
- **Relations with England**
    - The English Parliament, worried about Scotland's economic struggles and potential alliances with foreign powers, began discussing a formal union of the kingdoms. Many Scots, still bitter over the Darien fiasco, were wary. Meanwhile, others believed a union might open English colonial markets to Scottish merchants, preventing further fiascos.

Thus, as William's reign advanced, Scotland remained a separate kingdom governed by its own Parliament but increasingly entangled in joint British interests. With Mary's death in 1694 and William's passing in 1702, the monarchy passed to Queen Anne, another Protestant Stewart who supported deeper integration between England and Scotland.

---

6. Anne's Reign and the Move Toward Union (1702–1707)

Queen Anne (1702–1714) was the last Stewart monarch to preside over a separate Scottish crown before the Acts of Union. Her reign saw fresh Jacobite rumblings and a concerted push to unite Scotland and England legally:

- **Act of Security (1704)**
    - The Scottish Parliament, nervous about the English Act of Settlement (1701), which named the Protestant House of Hanover as heirs, passed the Act of Security. This measure declared that Scotland would choose its own successor after Anne, potentially a different dynasty from England, unless certain economic freedoms were granted.
    - England responded with the Alien Act (1705), threatening to treat Scots as aliens in England and block Scottish trade unless they negotiated union or accepted Hanoverian succession. Faced with crippling trade barriers, Scottish commissioners engaged in union talks.
- **Acts of Union (1707)**
    - After intense debates, the Scottish Parliament voted for an incorporating union with England. The majority was persuaded by financial benefits, including relief for the Darien investors (the "Equivalent" payment) and access to English colonial markets.
    - The Acts of Union came into effect on 1 May 1707, dissolving the Scottish Parliament and sending Scottish representatives to a new Parliament of Great Britain in Westminster. Scotland retained its distinct legal system, church (Presbyterian), and educational traditions, but lost an independent legislature and direct monarchy.

Many ordinary Scots felt ambivalent or hostile, seeing union as a surrender of sovereignty. In the Highlands, disaffected clans, often with Jacobite sympathies, grumbled about the "bought and sold for English gold" outcome. Yet for others, union promised economic revival and the security of Protestant succession.

7. The Jacobite Cause Under Anne and Beyond

Though the union settled certain constitutional questions, it did not extinguish Stuart (Stewart) claims to the throne. The exiled James Francis Edward Stuart (the "Old Pretender"), son of James VII, found support among Scots who yearned for a Stewart restoration:

- **Queen Anne's Succession**
    - Upon Anne's death in 1714, the throne of Great Britain passed to George I of Hanover, in accordance with the English Act of Settlement (extended to Scotland post-Union). Many Scots disliked the idea of a distant German-speaking monarch and saw a chance for the "rightful" Stewart heir, James, to press his claim.
- **1715 Jacobite Rising ("the Fifteen")**
    - Shortly after George I's accession, the Earl of Mar ("Bobbin' John") led Highland clans in a revolt, proclaiming James Francis Edward Stuart as King James VIII and III. The rebellion gained ground in the northeast, capturing Perth, but lacked robust nationwide support.
    - Government forces checked the Jacobites at the Battle of Sheriffmuir (November 1715), a confused stalemate that effectively ended the rising. James arrived in Scotland too late, finding the cause in disarray. He fled back to exile, leaving the attempt a failure.
- **Aftermath**
    - The government confiscated estates from rebel clans, installing loyal officials to oversee them. Yet the Hanoverian regime took a conciliatory tone, hoping not to provoke further unrest. Some clan leaders quietly nursed grievances, awaiting a better opportunity.

Though the 1715 rising failed, it signaled that the Jacobite cause—loyalty to the exiled Stewart line—remained potent in parts of Scotland. Another major rising would occur in 1745 under Charles Edward Stuart ("Bonnie Prince Charlie"), but that lies slightly beyond our current timeline. For now, it was clear that union did not unify Scottish hearts, especially in Gaelic Highlands where clan loyalties, Catholic or Episcopalian traditions, and historical attachments to the Stewart monarchy endured.

8. Shifts in Religious and Political Landscapes after 1707

The new British state created by the 1707 Union had to balance distinct religious settlements in Scotland and England:

- **Presbyterian Kirk Ascendant**
    - The Union guaranteed the Presbyterian system in Scotland's Church. Bishops had no official role, though Episcopalian congregations persisted in certain areas, often allied with Jacobite interests.
    - The Kirk's General Assembly continued to manage doctrinal and disciplinary matters, though tensions arose over "patronage"—the right of local landowners to present ministers. This issue caused controversies among ministers and elders who wanted a more grassroots selection process.
- **Cultural Cross-Currents**
    - Some Scots embraced the new British identity, forging commercial and intellectual ties with England's expanding empire. Edinburgh's cultural blossoming in the 18th century ("the Scottish Enlightenment") was partly funded by trade expansions.
    - Others, especially in the Highlands, found union less beneficial, feeling marginalized by Lowland elites who dominated the new British frameworks. Gaelic communities faced assimilation pressures, leading to future tensions that would erupt more dramatically after the 1745 Jacobite rising and the subsequent government crackdowns.
- **Hanoverian Stability vs. Jacobite Romanticism**
    - As the 18th century advanced, the Hanoverian regime consolidated, offering relative peace and improved trade for many Lowlanders. Yet the memory of the old Stewart line, fueled by clan tradition, Catholic hopes, and dissatisfaction with London-centric politics, preserved the Jacobite myth in Gaelic culture. Poets and bards lamented the exiled "King Over the Water," weaving a romantic narrative of lost Highland glory.

Thus, the Glorious Revolution and subsequent union shaped a British monarchy anchored in Protestant succession, imposing new definitions of loyalty. For most Scots, acceptance of the Hanoverian crown became the norm, but a significant minority maintained Stewart loyalties, culminating in further risings. Even beyond the immediate rebellions, these divisions influenced Scotland's cultural self-image, torn between assimilation into a larger British project and the lingering pull of ancestral Stewart allegiances.

---

9. Broader Implications of the Glorious Revolution in Scotland

Scotland's role in the Glorious Revolution and the subsequent union carried far-reaching consequences:

1. **Constitutional Ideas**
   - The Claim of Right (1689) articulated that a king who violated fundamental laws or attempted to reintroduce Catholicism could be lawfully deposed. This principle paralleled English revolutionary ideologies, bolstering the notion that monarchy was conditional on respecting Protestant liberties.
2. **Religious Pluralism and Regionalism**
   - Officially, Presbyterianism reigned in the Kirk, but Episcopalians and Catholics continued in certain enclaves—Highland glens, some Lowland parishes, or noble households. The government balanced harsh penal laws with sporadic leniency to avoid outright alienation of these minorities.
3. **Integration vs. Alienation**
   - For Lowland merchants and landowners seeking access to English markets, the union was a pragmatic success. They collaborated in the British Empire's expansion, forging business ventures in the colonies.
   - Contrastingly, many Highlanders felt excluded from the new order, fueling Gaelic discontent that shaped the Jacobite cause and produced future rebellions.
4. **Military and Political Structures**
   - The British state established a standing army that included Scottish regiments, diminishing the autonomy of

clan-based military power. Over time, some Highland chiefs integrated by serving as officers in British regiments, forging new loyalties.

Hence, the Glorious Revolution embedded the principle of a Protestant succession and guaranteed the Presbyterian Kirk, while the subsequent union sealed Scotland's absorption into a larger Anglo-centric framework. Jacobite risings were direct challenges to this arrangement, but they also contained deeper cultural dimensions—Highland traditions, dynastic loyalties, and a lingering sense that the rightful Stewart monarchy lived on in exile.

---

10. Conclusion

The Glorious Revolution in Scotland, culminating in the overthrow of James VII in 1689 and the installation of William and Mary, realigned the kingdom's religious and political structures. Presbyterian governance of the Kirk was restored, and a new wave of Jacobite loyalism emerged among those who refused to abandon the exiled Catholic monarch. Although an initial Jacobite rising flared in 1689–1691, the government's harsh measures subdued most clans, leaving behind pockets of bitterness epitomized by the Glencoe Massacre.

Subsequent economic strains—like the failure of the Darien Scheme—further convinced some Scottish elites to accept an incorporating union with England in 1707, hoping for commercial benefits and security of the Protestant succession. Yet union did not quell the Jacobite spirit, leading to future uprisings in 1715 and 1745. The final outcome was a Scotland increasingly tied to Britain's expanding empire, but also mindful of its own church settlement and cultural heritage.

Now, having explored the Glorious Revolution and the early Jacobite period, we see how the stage was set for the 18th-century transformations—enlightenment thought, deeper integration with Britain, and lingering Highland discontent. The interplay between these forces would shape Scotland's subsequent history, forging the paradoxical blend of a distinct national identity within a larger united kingdom that persists into more recent centuries.

CHAPTER 17

THE ACTS OF UNION 1707 AND CHANGING IDENTITIES

1. Introduction

By the dawn of the 18th century, Scotland remained a distinct kingdom under the Stuart (Stewart) line but was increasingly interwoven with England through a shared monarch and parallel religious upheavals. The Glorious Revolution (1688–1689) in Scotland had replaced James VII with William and Mary, securing a Presbyterian settlement for the Church of Scotland. However, financial turmoil—exemplified by the catastrophic Darien Scheme—and fears surrounding succession after Queen Anne's reign led many Scottish elites to contemplate a closer constitutional union with England.

In 1706–1707, amid heated debates, commissioners from Scotland and England negotiated the Acts of Union. These statutes united the two realms into the new state of Great Britain, dissolving Scotland's independent Parliament but preserving certain institutional pillars like Scots law and the Presbyterian Kirk. This chapter explores the complex motivations behind the union, the vehement opposition and popular unrest, the final passage of the Acts, and the far-reaching changes in Scottish identities that ensued. We will also examine how this new constitutional arrangement transformed trade, politics, social relations, and set the stage for future economic and cultural developments that would reshape the nation.

---

2. Background: The Road to Formal Union

Although James VI had become James I of England in 1603, that was only a *personal* union—Scotland and England remained separate states, each with its own parliament, laws, and church. Nonetheless, subsequent decades saw:

1. **Increased Political Entanglement**

- Through the 17th century, the two kingdoms' policies converged around the Stuart monarchy. The Civil Wars and Cromwellian occupation disrupted national boundaries, and after the Restoration in 1660, the crown attempted to manage both parliaments according to royal priorities.
- Meanwhile, tensions lingered: many English politicians disliked dealing with a separate Scottish realm that might choose a different successor if the throne became vacant, while Scots resented being overshadowed by England.

2. **Succession Uncertainty**
    - The English Act of Settlement (1701) named the Protestant House of Hanover as heirs in England should Queen Anne die childless. Scottish leaders feared losing the autonomy to choose their own monarch. The Scottish Parliament responded with the Act of Security (1704), suggesting Scotland *could* select a different monarch—perhaps a European ally or the exiled Stewart claimant—if England failed to respect Scottish interests.

3. **Economic Frustrations**
    - The late 17th century battered Scotland's economy. Failed harvests in the 1690s caused widespread famine ("the seven ill years"). The disastrous Darien Scheme (1695–1700), in which Scots poured resources into an unsuccessful colonial settlement in Panama, exacerbated financial ruin.
    - Many Scots blamed England for undermining Darien—English merchants and the East India Company had indeed refused support—stoking anger. Yet the fiasco also convinced some that Scotland, lacking major colonies or strong maritime capacity, *needed* access to England's empire for survival.

4. **Alien Act (1705)**
    - In response to Scotland's Act of Security, the English Parliament passed the Alien Act, threatening to treat Scots as *aliens* in England if no steps toward union or a shared succession were taken. It also threatened to bar Scottish trade with English colonies. This placed immense pressure on Scotland's economy, which relied on cross-border and Atlantic commerce.

Amid these forces—succession fears, financial desperation, and English economic leverage—the stage was set for formal negotiations to create a single unified state.

---

3. The Treaty of Union Negotiations (1706)

In April 1706, commissioners from both kingdoms convened in London to discuss terms. The Scots included figures like the Duke of Queensberry (High Commissioner) and John Campbell, Duke of Argyll; on the English side were prominent political leaders such as Lord Godolphin and Robert Harley. Their key objectives included:

- **England's Goals**
    - Secure the Protestant succession across Britain.
    - Prevent Scotland from forging separate alliances that could threaten English security.
    - End the possibility of an independent Scottish foreign policy or monarchy.
    - Gain stable control over the entire island's trade and defense.
- **Scotland's Goals**
    - Guarantee the Presbyterian Church settlement.
    - Protect Scots law and the Scottish legal courts from English interference.
    - Obtain an "Equivalent" payment to offset the debts and losses of the Darien investors.
    - Secure access to English (and colonial) markets for Scottish merchants.

By summer's end, the commissioners reached a draft treaty of 25 articles. Major provisions included:

1. **Union of Parliaments**:
    - Scotland's Parliament and England's Parliament dissolved in favor of a new Parliament of Great Britain at Westminster. Forty-five MPs would represent Scottish constituencies in

the House of Commons, alongside 16 Scottish peers in the House of Lords.
2. **Succession**:
    - The Protestant line of Hanover would inherit both thrones, ensuring one sovereign for "Great Britain."
3. **Equivalent Payment**:
    - Scotland would receive a lump sum ("the Equivalent") to compensate for inheriting a share of England's national debt and to reimburse Darien shareholders. This was around £398,085 at the time—an enormous figure for the Scottish economy.
4. **Safeguards for the Kirk and Scots Law**:
    - Articles guaranteed the Presbyterian Church in Scotland and upheld the separate legal system. They also preserved Scottish universities and stated that no English religious tests would disqualify Scots from certain offices.

---

4. Fierce Debates in the Scottish Parliament

Once the draft treaty reached Edinburgh in October 1706, the Scottish Parliament ignited with controversy. The debate ran from October 1706 to January 1707. Key factions included:

- **Court Party (Pro-Union)**
    - Led by Queensberry, Argyll, and other nobles who had close ties to the monarchy. They argued that union would secure the Protestant line, remove the threat of English sanctions, and open vast trade opportunities. Many were influenced by the promise of Equivalent money and potential personal rewards (titles, offices, etc.).
    - This group contended that the risk of continuing separately—especially with the possibility of a Jacobite or rival dynasty—was too high.
- **Country Party (Anti-Union)**
    - Figures like Andrew Fletcher of Saltoun, Hamilton, and many others who deplored the idea of losing Scottish

sovereignty. They warned that dissolving Parliament would reduce Scotland to a province of England.
    - Popular pamphlets labeled union as a "selling of the nation," evoking patriotism and concern that the Presbyterian faith would still be overshadowed by the larger Anglican majority in the new British Parliament.
- **Popular Unrest**
    - Outside Parliament, crowds in Edinburgh, Glasgow, and elsewhere demonstrated against the treaty. Protesters burned effigies and threatened union supporters. Royal troops guarded the Parliament House in Edinburgh to prevent riots.
    - Petitions poured in from shires, burghs, and church presbyteries, many condemning union. However, the government majority in Parliament, backed by royal authority, persisted.

Despite the public outcry, article by article, the pro-union bloc won votes in Parliament. Subsidies, patronage, and unwavering support from Queen Anne's ministers ensured that enough members were swayed or silenced. On 16 January 1707, the final ratification bill passed: 110 votes in favor, 69 against. Resistance eventually subsided, though bitterness lingered.

---

5. The Final Acts: 1 May 1707

With both parliaments approving the articles, the union formally took effect on 1 May 1707, creating the new Kingdom of Great Britain. Key outcomes:

- **The End of the Old Parliament**
    - Scotland's last independent Parliament adjourned in March 1707. Some members wept; others saw it as a necessary sacrifice. The next legislative body representing Scots would be in London, with a small contingent of peers and commoners.

- - Though Scots retained their separate courts and laws, the legislative power to change these laws now rested with Westminster.
- **British Parliament Representation**
  - Out of around 558 English MPs, only 45 were designated for Scottish constituencies, plus 16 Scottish peers in the Lords. Critics argued this was minimal representation—especially given England's far larger population. Nonetheless, it gave Scots an official voice in the imperial parliament for the first time.
- **Preservation of the Kirk**
  - Despite concerns, the Church of Scotland remained Presbyterian, protected by the "Act for Securing the Protestant Religion and Presbyterian Church Government." This proved essential for calming clergy's fears of an Anglican takeover.
- **Economic Hopes and Uncertainties**
  - The Equivalent was disbursed, offering partial compensation to Darien shareholders and the Scottish treasury. Yet many ordinary Scots wondered if new tax burdens (aligned with England's system) would outweigh any trade benefits.
  - Some merchants eagerly pursued opportunities in England's colonial markets, while rural folk worried about potential competition from English goods or about farmland changes.

In the short term, anti-Union sentiment remained strong among the populace. Many predicted that Scotland's national identity would wither. Others, particularly in commercial circles, believed prosperity awaited under a unified empire. Time would tell which view prevailed.

---

6. Popular Reaction and Identity Shifts

In the immediate aftermath, disillusion dominated many corners of Scottish society:

- **National Symbolism**
  - Scotland's Crown, Sceptre, and Sword of State were no longer used for domestic coronations, though they remained national relics in Edinburgh Castle. Some Scots felt a sense of bereavement at losing an independent monarchy.
- **Jacobite Potential**
  - Jacobites capitalized on discontent, claiming the union was illegitimate and orchestrated by bribery. The exiled James Francis Edward Stuart ("the Old Pretender") could appeal to patriots who despised Westminster rule. The 1708 attempted French-backed invasion was partly an effort to exploit anti-Union anger, though it failed.
- **Economic Mixed Results**
  - In the early years, integration was slow. Some industries, like linen and cattle, found new markets, eventually thriving in the decades ahead. Others, especially small-scale burgh crafts, struggled to compete with English producers.
  - Over time, major Lowland towns (Glasgow, Edinburgh, Aberdeen) began reorienting trade routes to the Americas, spurring merchant wealth. This contributed to the growth of an urban middle class that would drive intellectual and cultural movements (like the Enlightenment).
- **Cultural Adaptation**
  - At the elite level, some Scots aristocrats moved to London, seeking court patronage, or joined the British Army and Navy, rising within imperial ranks. This integration created a new "British" aristocracy with Scottish roots.
  - Meanwhile, Gaelic-speaking Highlands largely remained apart from these developments, continuing clan traditions and chafing under additional taxes or centralized regulation. Here, the sense of being "sold out" by Lowland elites fueled future Jacobite sympathy.

Gradually, Scots navigated a dual identity: participants in the growing British empire yet maintaining distinct legal, educational, and religious institutions. The tension between "Britishness" and "Scottishness" would become a hallmark of the 18th century.

7. Political Landscape Post-Union

Despite the union, political life in Scotland did not vanish. It simply shifted forms:

1. **The Scottish Representative Peers and MPs**
    - Every new parliament at Westminster elected 16 representative peers from Scotland's noble ranks. The 45 Scottish MPs in the House of Commons varied in outlook—some supported government policies to protect or expand trade; others were anti-government or Jacobite-leaning.
    - Over time, blocs formed: some loyal to the government ("Court Party") seeking British appointments, others ("Patriots") advocating for Scottish concerns or opposing corruption.
2. **Rise of Patronage Networks**
    - Without a domestic parliament, Scottish aristocrats and lairds jockeyed for influence through the Secretary of State for Scotland (initially) or direct royal favor at London. Patronage determined who secured lucrative posts or local offices.
    - This phenomenon led to "managed elections," where powerful magnates controlled burgh or county constituencies. Critics lamented that genuine popular representation was rare.
3. **Jacobite Undercurrent**
    - Though overt rebellion was dampened post-1708, sporadic plots continued. Government spies kept watch on known Jacobite sympathizers. Some wealthier landowners quietly paid lip service to the Hanoverian regime while secretly contributing to Jacobite funds.
    - French intrigue also persisted, with Stuart exiles in France seeking a favorable political moment to return.

Thus, while the union centralized ultimate legislative power in Westminster, it also fostered new alliances and feuds among Scottish elites who tried to advance local interests in a British framework. Over time, a stable group of Scottish MPs emerged at Westminster, forging cross-border connections that gradually integrated political cultures.

---

8. Economic Evolution and Early Enlightenment Links

By the mid-18th century, the union's economic impact became more apparent:

- **Glasgow's Tobacco Trade**
    - One significant success story was Glasgow's surge as a hub for importing tobacco from the American colonies. Previously marginalized by the Navigation Acts, Scots merchants now accessed colonial markets as British subjects, leading to rapid wealth accumulation in southwestern ports.
    - This mercantile prosperity funded urban development: grand townhouses, new squares, and philanthropic ventures. Glasgow's "Tobacco Lords" became influential voices in shaping Scottish commerce and opinion.
- **Edinburgh as a Cultural Center**
    - Though no longer the seat of an independent parliament, Edinburgh's elite turned their energies to intellectual pursuits, forming clubs, societies, and salons that discussed philosophy, science, and literature.
    - This environment catalyzed what would soon be hailed as the Scottish Enlightenment—a remarkable flowering of ideas that combined rational inquiry, moral philosophy, economic theories, and critiques of aristocratic mores.
- **Agricultural and Industrial Beginnings**
    - In rural Lowlands, "Improvement" ideas spread, encouraging better farming techniques, crop rotations, enclosures, and the adoption of new livestock breeds. Though not fully realized in the early 18th century, these innovations laid groundwork for an agricultural revolution.
    - Early textile manufacturing expanded around linen, with impetus from the Board of Trustees for Fisheries and

Manufactures (founded 1727). This proto-industrial growth would accelerate later in the century.

Culturally, a sense of optimism grew among certain urban elites who felt that union, despite initial pains, was delivering commercial benefits. Meanwhile, intellectual ferment in Edinburgh and other burghs nurtured a distinctive Scottish perspective on universal Enlightenment themes.

---

9. Continued Jacobite Threat and the 1719 Rising

Even as some Lowland regions prospered, discontent endured in the Highlands:

- **Spanish Intervention (1719)**
    - After the failed 1715 rising, exiled Jacobites sought allies abroad. Spain, at odds with Britain over Mediterranean trade and colonial disputes, decided to sponsor a small-scale Jacobite expedition to the western Highlands.
    - The rising was poorly coordinated, landing near Eilean Donan Castle. Spanish troops supported a handful of clans, but the enterprise collapsed at the Battle of Glen Shiel (June 1719). British government forces swiftly suppressed the incursion.

Though minor, the 1719 episode underlined that the Jacobite cause was not extinguished. Highland clans aligned with Catholic or Episcopalian traditions remained open to restoring the Stuarts, while the British government's hold on northern territories was incomplete.

---

10. Eighteenth-Century Social Transformations

The early decades of union brought shifts in social hierarchy and mobility:

1. **Ennobled Families**

- Some Scottish noble houses intermarried with English peers, forging a British aristocracy. Young heirs spent more time in London, adopting English manners and tastes. This cultural assimilation sometimes widened the gap between aristocrats and their local tenants.

2. **Middle-Class Growth**
    - Burgh merchants, professionals, and clerics thrived amid increased trade, improved schooling, and access to new ideas. These individuals formed clubs like the Speculative Society or the Select Society in Edinburgh, preludes to the Enlightenment.

3. **Highland vs. Lowland Divergence**
    - The Highlands, governed by clan chiefs, saw fewer direct benefits from union. Gaelic culture continued largely outside the new commercial networks. Clans that maintained Jacobite loyalty or Catholic faith felt especially marginalized.
    - Government presence in the Highlands was sporadic; some roads were built under General Wade after the 1715 rising, but the region's social fabric was still predominantly clan-based, setting the stage for future confrontation.

4. **Religious Variations**
    - The Kirk, now established officially as Presbyterian, wrestled with internal factionalism: moderates vs. evangelicals (the "Marrow Controversy" of the 1710s–1720s, etc.). Secessions by stricter ministers formed smaller Presbyterian bodies.
    - In the northeast and certain pockets, Episcopalian worship persisted, often allied with latent Jacobitism. Catholics survived primarily in parts of the Highlands and western isles, tolerated but occasionally persecuted.

Hence, the post-Union era was no monolith: some embraced the opportunities of British integration, others felt dispossessed. The interplay between these attitudes shaped the cultural matrix that would soon spark Scotland's intellectual golden age.

11. Intellectual Undercurrents: Pre-Enlightenment Stirrings

Before the "Scottish Enlightenment" fully blossomed (usually dated from the 1740s onward), seeds of philosophical and scientific inquiry were taking root:

- **Universities and Academics**
    - Scotland's universities (St Andrews, Glasgow, Aberdeen, and Edinburgh) reformed curricula. Professors introduced Newtonian physics and Cartesian philosophy, encouraging critical thinking.
    - Scholars like Colin Maclaurin (mathematician in Edinburgh) and Robert Sibbald (natural historian) paved the way for advanced research. Maclaurin, for instance, was a protégé of Isaac Newton, demonstrating cross-British intellectual ties.
- **Literary Societies and Periodicals**
    - Literary clubs, coffeehouses, and periodical journals appeared, disseminating new ideas. Writers debated political economy, moral philosophy, and theological controversies.
    - The Union's expansion of trade networks also facilitated the import of European books and the exchange of letters with continental thinkers, laying a cosmopolitan foundation that would flourish under Enlightenment luminaries like David Hume and Adam Smith.
- **Secular Critiques of Authority**
    - While the Kirk retained significant moral authority, a younger generation of scholars began questioning dogmatic positions. This was not outright atheism but a shift toward reasoned debate about scripture, ethics, and the nature of governance.
    - The legal profession likewise expanded, with advocates in Edinburgh's Parliament House applying rational methods to jurisprudence, bridging Scots law's unique traditions with broader European legal thought.

Thus, though overshadowed by political tensions, an undercurrent of intellectual renewal was stirring in early 18th-century Scotland, fueled by the union's broader horizons and by persistent national introspection about Scotland's distinctiveness within Britain.

12. Conclusion

The Acts of Union in 1707 stand as a pivotal moment in Scottish history, dissolving the old Parliament and merging the kingdom with England to form Great Britain. Despite fierce opposition and widespread public dismay, the union proceeded—driven by economic pressures, diplomatic maneuvers, and the promise of securing the Protestant succession. In the immediate decades, Scotland experienced both the benefits and trials of integration: merchant wealth grew in port cities, new market opportunities arose, but the Jacobite cause simmered in the Highlands, culminating in further uprisings.

At the same time, political representation shifted to Westminster, forging new patronage networks and reorienting elite ambitions. Many Scots adapted, finding roles in imperial commerce or the British military. Others clung to older loyalties or nursed resentments, especially in Gaelic territories. Against this backdrop, an intellectual awakening quietly gained momentum, setting the stage for the remarkable Scottish Enlightenment. In the next chapter, we will delve into that cultural efflorescence, exploring how thinkers like Hume, Smith, and others reinvented philosophy, economics, and science, shaping the modern world from the heart of 18th-century Scotland.

CHAPTER 18

THE SCOTTISH ENLIGHTENMENT

1. Introduction

The mid- to late-18th century saw Scotland emerge as a major center of intellectual and cultural innovation. This epoch, commonly termed the "Scottish Enlightenment," featured philosophers, economists, historians, scientists, and literary figures whose works influenced Western thought profoundly. Thinkers such as David Hume, Adam Smith, and Thomas Reid proposed groundbreaking ideas about human nature, moral philosophy, political economy, and empirical science. Their success did not occur in a vacuum: it was fostered by Scotland's unique social context post-Union, the country's robust educational tradition, expanding urban life, and the impetus to reconcile "Scottishness" within a larger British framework.

In this chapter, we explore the origins, principal actors, key ideas, and social environments of the Scottish Enlightenment. We will see how universities, clubs, and patronage networks shaped an intellectual community that prized reason, skepticism, and civic virtue—while simultaneously grappling with the legacy of religious disputes and the quest for a modern commercial society. By examining these thinkers' contributions and the controversies they faced, we can appreciate how Scotland wielded an outsized influence on Enlightenment-era debates throughout Europe and the transatlantic world.

---

2. Foundations: Education and Urban Networks

Several structural pillars underpinned Scotland's Enlightenment:

- **A Reformed University System**
    - Scotland's ancient universities—St Andrews, Glasgow, Aberdeen, and Edinburgh—had each weathered the Reformation and subsequent religious upheavals. By the early 18th century, they pivoted toward more secular

curricula, emphasizing mathematics, natural philosophy (science), and moral philosophy. Professors were freer to explore new theories, especially after the union loosened direct ecclesiastical or aristocratic control.
    - Chairs in moral philosophy and logic gained prominence. Pioneering figures developed courses that integrated Newtonian physics, Cartesian reasoning, and moral-sense theories.
- **Urban Cosmopolitanism**
    - Edinburgh, though no longer home to an independent parliament, retained a concentration of lawyers, judges, and clergy, fueling a culture of debate in taverns, coffeehouses, and clubs. The city's "New Town," developed from the 1760s onward, symbolized aspirations for modernity and rational design.
    - Glasgow's prosperity from tobacco and other colonial trades funded scholarly and civic projects, while Aberdeen boasted active intellectual communities around its colleges. Rapid urban growth allowed for the cross-pollination of ideas among merchants, professors, and literati.
- **Clubs and Societies**
    - Membership-driven clubs like the Select Society, the Philosophical Society of Edinburgh, and the Edinburgh Literary Society offered forums where thinkers read papers, critiqued each other's arguments, and refined their works.
    - Gentlemen's clubs, Masonic lodges, and informal drawing-room gatherings also promoted social exchange, bridging backgrounds. A laird from the Highlands might meet a Lowland merchant or an English traveler, generating cosmopolitan dialogues.

This environment cultivated a synergy between practical reforms (e.g., improving agriculture, rationalizing law) and theoretical discourse, as intellectuals sought to apply reason to social betterment.

3. Key Figures and Their Contributions

David Hume (1711–1776)

- **Philosophy and Empiricism**
    - Arguably the Enlightenment's most influential Scottish philosopher, Hume championed a radical empirical approach. In his *Treatise of Human Nature* (1739–1740), he dissected human knowledge, arguing that ideas derive from sense impressions. He questioned the certainty of causation and the concept of a stable self-identity.
    - Hume's skepticism was controversial. Religious conservatives saw him as undercutting proofs of God's existence, and he faced difficulties securing a university post. Yet his works, including *An Enquiry Concerning Human Understanding* (1748), shaped modern epistemology.
- **Moral Psychology and History**
    - Hume believed moral judgments derived from sentiment—an innate "moral sense"—rather than pure reason. This idea, that passion drives ethics, influenced moral philosophy for generations.
    - His *History of England* offered a narrative guided by rational analysis rather than providential interpretation, exemplifying an Enlightenment approach to historiography.

Adam Smith (1723–1790)

- **Political Economy**
    - Often hailed as the "father of economics," Smith's *An Inquiry into the Nature and Causes of the Wealth of Nations* (1776) revolutionized understandings of commerce and governance. He advocated for free markets guided by self-interest and "the invisible hand," though he also supported state roles like education, infrastructure, and justice.
- **Moral Philosophy**
    - Before *Wealth of Nations*, Smith penned *The Theory of Moral Sentiments* (1759), arguing that sympathy (or empathy) underpins moral judgments. Through "the impartial

spectator," individuals gauge right and wrong. This integrated well with Hume's sentiment-based ethics, though Smith emphasized social relationships and moral faculties.

Thomas Reid (1710–1796)

- **Common Sense Philosophy**
    - Reacting against Hume's skepticism, Reid developed the "philosophy of common sense." He asserted that humans possess inherent faculties—like perception, memory, and moral intuition—that yield reliable knowledge of the external world.
    - Reid's ideas profoundly influenced later Anglo-American philosophy, offering an alternative to radical empiricism.

Others

- **Francis Hutcheson (1694–1746)**: A pioneer of moral sense theory, inspiring both Hume and Smith.
- **Hugh Blair (1718–1800)**: A minister and rhetorician, famous for his lectures on literature and eloquence, shaping modern English prose style.
- **William Robertson (1721–1793)**: A historian who wrote widely read works on Scotland, America, and the reign of Charles V, applying Enlightenment rationality to historical narratives.
- **John Home (1722–1808)**: Playwright known for the tragic drama *Douglas*, signifying a blossoming of Scottish literary culture.

These interconnected figures shared personal friendships, corresponded frequently, and tested each other's theories in societies and clubs. Their synergy made the Scottish Enlightenment remarkable for both its cohesive intellectual community and wide-ranging impact.

4. The Role of Religion and Moderation

Although many Enlightenment thinkers questioned dogma, the movement did not wholly reject Christianity. Instead, it often sought a more tolerant, rational faith:

- **Moderate vs. Evangelical Wings**
    - The Kirk, still Presbyterian, was split. "Moderates" embraced polite learning, minimal doctrinal strife, and broad cultural engagement. Ministers like Hugh Blair exemplified this stance, championing moral edification over strict Calvinist fervor.
    - "Evangelicals" or "High Flyers" believed in more rigorous theology, emphasizing personal conversion and scriptural authority. They frowned on the philosophes' worldliness. Conflict over patronage in parish appointments highlighted these rifts.
- **Secularization of Public Discourse**
    - Coffeehouses and clubs offered spaces where theology was not dominant, replaced by reason-based debate on politics, economics, and aesthetics. A new moral philosophy separate from strict confessional boundaries emerged, enabling cooperation among men of diverse religious persuasions.
- **Debates on Tolerance**
    - Enlightenment authors generally supported tolerance for religious dissent, viewing sectarian persecution as a relic of barbarity. Yet, in practice, full tolerance for Catholics or certain radical sects remained elusive, given lingering fears from the Jacobite era.

This moderate religious climate fostered an environment in which reason and sociability could flourish without immediate censure, setting Scottish intellectuals apart from more polarized contexts on the continent.

5. Social and Economic Context of Ideas

The blossoming of the Scottish Enlightenment was intertwined with evolving social structures:

1. **Increasingly Commercial Society**
    - Smith's *Wealth of Nations* dovetailed with real changes in trade, as Glasgow merchants dominated tobacco imports and, later, re-exported it to Europe. The profits supported philanthropic societies, libraries, and academic endowments.
    - Debates about free trade, colonization, and the moral implications of commerce engaged thinkers. Some recognized the contradictions in moral philosophy and the rising Atlantic slave trade, though direct critiques of slavery would be more forceful in the late 18th century.
2. **Agricultural Improvements**
    - Enclosing fields, improving drainage, and introducing new crops (e.g., turnips, clover) transformed Lowland estates. Landlords often engaged in "rational" estate management, inspired by Enlightenment treatises on agriculture.
    - Such changes displaced some small tenants but also boosted productivity, tying into Enlightenment debates on modernization and the "progress of society."
3. **Urban Living and Polite Society**
    - Town dwellers participated in assemblies, dancing clubs, music societies, and societies for the improvement of manners. Edinburg's New Town design (largely credited to James Craig's plan in 1767) exemplified rational geometric layouts.
    - Politeness, refinement, and civility became watchwords, reflecting Enlightenment emphasis on social harmony. Yet critiques of superficial luxury circulated, echoing republican ideals of civic virtue.

In short, the interplay between rising commerce, urban sophistication, and agricultural transformation fed the intellectual impetus to examine how societies progressed, how wealth was created, and what moral obligations society owed its members.

6. Impact and Reception in Europe

Scottish thinkers did not confine their influence to Britain:

- **Continental Engagement**
    - Translations of Hume's and Smith's works appeared in French, German, Italian, and beyond. European philosophes admired Scotland as a place of advanced education unburdened by the stifling structures of absolute monarchy.
    - Voltaire, the French Enlightenment luminary, praised Scottish intellectual vibrancy. Hume spent time in France, forging friendships with figures like Jean-Jacques Rousseau (though their relationship ended badly). This cross-pollination linked the Scottish Enlightenment to broader continental movements.
- **Inspiring American Thinkers**
    - Scottish ideas greatly influenced the American colonies, especially moral sense theory and economic liberalism. Many colonial leaders, such as John Witherspoon (a Scottish clergyman who became President of Princeton), carried Scottish Enlightenment perspectives to the American founding.
    - The concept of a "natural liberty" combined with moderate Presbyterian teachings resonated with certain American patriots, shaping Revolutionary-era discourses on rights and governance.
- **Critiques Abroad**
    - Not all embraced the Scots. Some Catholic strongholds viewed them as dangerously skeptical or heretical. Hardcore conservatives equated the Scots' brand of rational religion with potential moral relativism. Nonetheless, the broad respect for Scottish scholarship remained notable.

Thus, the Scottish Enlightenment contributed significantly to the Age of Reason's global conversation. Themes of empiricism, moral sentiment, historical analysis, and political economy found receptive audiences well beyond the High Street of Edinburgh.

7. Late-Century Developments: Shifting Tides

By the 1770s–1780s, the Scottish Enlightenment began to evolve:

1. **Rise of Younger Generation**
   - Authors like James Boswell (1740–1795) bridged the gap between Scottish intellectual circles and London's literary scene, famously chronicling his friendship with Samuel Johnson. Lord Kames (Henry Home), Adam Ferguson, and John Millar contributed to the "science of man," analyzing historical and social processes with new rigor.
   - These scholars further advanced theories of societal progress, linking anthropology, law, and moral philosophy.
2. **Critiques of Enlightenment Orthodoxy**
   - Some Presbyterians warned that the movement's rational tendencies diluted genuine faith. They feared a slide toward deism or irreligion. Robert Burns (1759–1796), the national poet, embodied a tension between Enlightenment humanism and popular Scots tradition, often challenging clerical hypocrisy in his verses.
   - On the political front, radical Whig ideas—spurred by the American Revolution (1776) and later the French Revolution (1789)—disturbed moderate Scottish literati, who prized stability but also recognized calls for broader representation and liberty.
3. **Growing British Identity**
   - Many Enlightenment thinkers embraced the expanding British Empire as a vehicle for progress and commercial growth. Yet a distinctly Scottish pride persisted—rooted in the distinct legacy of the Kirk, the separate legal system, and the memory of past achievements.
   - The Gaelic Highlands underwent profound changes (e.g., early Clearances, post-1745 clampdowns), continuing to highlight internal cultural divides. Enlightened Lowland intellectuals sometimes disparaged Gaelic customs as backward, illustrating the movement's ambivalent stance on cultural pluralism.

As the century closed, Enlightenment energies fed into questions about constitutional reform, colonial governance, and the role of reason versus tradition. Scotland's intellectual milieu kept producing influential theories, but signs of tension and transformation marked the end of this golden era.

8. Legacy and Influence on Modern Thought

The Scottish Enlightenment fundamentally shaped Western modernity. Its lasting contributions include:

1. **Moral Philosophy and Empiricism**
   - Hume's emphasis on experience and Reid's common-sense realism continue to underpin Anglo-American philosophy. Debates on skepticism, causation, and personal identity still reference Hume, while Reid's notion of intuitive knowledge influenced American pragmatism.
2. **Political Economy**
   - Adam Smith's classical economics became a cornerstone of liberal economic theory, informing subsequent thinkers such as David Ricardo, John Stuart Mill, and, later, Milton Friedman. The notion of free markets, division of labor, and self-regulation remains a bedrock of contemporary capitalist systems (though often critiqued).
3. **Historical and Sociological Approach**
   - Scottish historians and sociologists such as William Robertson, Adam Ferguson (*An Essay on the History of Civil Society*, 1767), and John Millar introduced systematic analyses of social development—anticipating later sociology and anthropology. They examined progress from "savage" to "civilized" societies (though couched in the Eurocentric terms of the time).
4. **Secular Ethical Perspectives**
   - The moral-sentiment approach (Hutcheson, Hume, Smith) championed virtues like sympathy, benevolence, and the moral sense. This outlook influenced Enlightenment deism, liberal Christianity, and eventually secular humanism, proposing that conscience and empathy guide ethical behavior independent of strict church authority.
5. **Educational and Civic Ideals**
   - Enlightenment Scots upheld universal education, intellectual debate, and civic improvement. Their emphasis on reasoned discussion in societies, clubs, and universities set standards for modern academic discourse and urban cultural life.

9. Conclusion

The Scottish Enlightenment stood as one of the 18th century's brightest intellectual movements, springing from a distinctive mix of post-Union circumstances, robust educational traditions, moderate religious frameworks, and a flourishing of urban social networks. Philosophers like David Hume, Adam Smith, Thomas Reid, and their contemporaries reshaped global discussions on knowledge, economics, morality, and history. Their debates over skepticism and common sense, free trade versus moral concerns, and the interplay of faith and reason reverberated far beyond Scotland's borders, influencing the American and French Revolutions and planting seeds for modern liberal thought.

Though internal tensions—religious divides, Jacobite memories, Highland versus Lowland disparities—lingered, the Enlightenment era endowed Scotland with a reputation for progressive learning and reasoned inquiry. This legacy persisted into subsequent centuries, even as industrial transformation and global empire-building began to dominate the national agenda. In our next chapters, we will examine how the Industrial Revolution, mass emigration, and evolving social reforms carried Scotland forward, all while echoing the intellectual spirit unleashed by these extraordinary 18th-century minds.

CHAPTER 19

THE IMPACT OF THE INDUSTRIAL REVOLUTION

1. Introduction

By the late 18th century, Scotland stood at the threshold of a profound economic and social transformation. The intellectual ferment of the Scottish Enlightenment had set the stage for new ways of thinking about science, innovation, and improvement, while the Acts of Union (1707) and subsequent access to British colonial markets provided broader commercial horizons. At the same time, Britain as a whole was undergoing dramatic changes in manufacturing and technology—an era now commonly called the Industrial Revolution. For Scotland, this revolution would manifest most visibly in the Lowland cities, where factories, mills, and mines proliferated. Yet it would also reach into rural districts, reshaping agricultural practices and prompting migrations into urban centers.

In this chapter, we explore how the Industrial Revolution unfolded in Scotland from roughly the mid-18th to the mid-19th centuries. We will look at key industries—textiles, iron and steel, coal mining, shipbuilding—and how they spurred urban growth in places like Glasgow, Lanarkshire, and the Lothians. We will examine the social consequences, from the emergence of a new working class and labor struggles to changes in family life, housing, and health. Finally, we will consider regional disparities, particularly the relative isolation of the Highlands from the industrial boom. Through this lens, we can see how Scotland's experiences contributed to both local identities and Britain's wider economic might, setting the foundation for modern industrial capitalism.

---

2. Preconditions for Industrial Growth

Scotland did not leap into industrialization overnight. A complex web of factors prepared the ground for mechanical and technological breakthroughs:

1. **Agricultural Improvements**
    - Starting in the late 17th and early 18th centuries, landowners and "improving" tenants introduced better crop rotations, drainage, enclosure, and new livestock breeds. These changes raised productivity, creating modest surpluses that supported a larger non-farming population.
    - Regions like East Lothian, the Borders, and parts of the northeast gained reputations for progressive farming. Greater efficiency freed some laborers to seek urban employment, fueling an emerging pool of wage workers.
2. **Access to Markets and Capital**
    - After the union with England, Scottish merchants participated more fully in imperial trade, notably with the Americas. Glasgow's tobacco lords exemplify this trend—amassing wealth through Atlantic commerce.
    - This merchant capital, alongside investments from landowners seeking new ventures, provided funds for early industrial experiments. Banks (like the Bank of Scotland, the Royal Bank of Scotland, and later local banks) expanded credit, facilitating entrepreneurial activity.
3. **Tradition of Skilled Crafts and Engineering**
    - Pre-industrial Scotland featured robust craft guilds in burghs, specializing in textiles, metalwork, and other trades. As Enlightenment-era institutions promoted scientific inquiry, engineers and tinkerers found encouragement to develop mechanical devices.
    - The existence of artisan communities in towns like Edinburgh, Perth, and Glasgow provided a foundation of technical know-how that could be repurposed for factory settings.
4. **Coal and Iron Deposits**
    - Central Scotland contained significant coalfields (the Central Belt, Fife, Lanarkshire, Lothians) and ironstone deposits. Early in the 18th century, the mining of coal for domestic heat and small-scale industry was already established.
    - As steam engines advanced, abundant local fuel sources lowered costs, giving central Scotland an edge in powering machinery and forging iron.

These foundations—agricultural surpluses, merchant capital, engineering capabilities, and natural resources—together positioned Scotland to capitalize on technological innovations that were gathering momentum across Britain.

3. Textile Manufacturing: From Cottage Industry to Mills

Textiles were among the earliest Scottish industries to experience mechanization, paralleling developments in northern England:

1. **Linen and Woolens Tradition**
    - Linen production had a long history in Scotland. Before industrialization, linen weaving was often a cottage craft, where families spun flax and wove cloth for local sale or small-scale export. Similarly, the woolen trade centered on weaving tweeds and other fabrics.
    - Government boards, like the Board of Trustees for Fisheries and Manufactures (established 1727), promoted improvements in linen quality, hoping to boost exports.
2. **Cotton Comes to Glasgow**
    - By the late 18th century, cotton supplanted linen in some Lowland regions because it was cheaper to produce and more versatile for mass markets. Entrepreneurs in Glasgow and Paisley imported raw cotton from the Americas, employing new spinning technologies (e.g., Arkwright's water frame, Hargreaves's spinning jenny).
    - The 1780s and 1790s saw the establishment of water-powered mills along the River Clyde and its tributaries, eventually transitioning to steam power. Paisley, famed for its shawls, boomed as a textile center.
3. **Factory System and Its Consequences**
    - Mechanization required large capital outlays for machinery and mill construction, shifting production from cottages to centralized factories. Workers, predominantly women and children, toiled for long hours under harsh discipline.
    - Skilled handloom weavers, once proud artisans, found themselves threatened by power-looms introduced in the

early 19th century. In places like Glasgow and Lanarkshire, handloom weavers' wages plummeted, sparking unrest and protest against mechanization.
4. **Growth of Urban Textile Centers**
    - Towns like Paisley, Dundee (noted for linen and, later, jute), and parts of Lanarkshire experienced rapid population growth. Mill owners built tenement housing near factories, resulting in crowded living conditions.
    - Child labor was common in cotton mills, prompting early moral and political debates about working conditions. These controversies would later feed into the 19th-century factory reform movements.

Cotton and linen mills thus spearheaded Scotland's factory-based economy, forging new social hierarchies between mill owners and laborers, while fueling urban expansion in the west and east coasts.

---

4. Iron, Steel, and Coal: The Industrial Heart

Beyond textiles, the extraction and processing of coal, iron, and later steel underpinned Scotland's industrial might:

1. **Coal Mining**
    - Scotland's coalfields, especially around the Forth-Clyde valley, had been worked for centuries. But steam-powered pumping engines (like those perfected by James Watt in the 1770s) permitted deeper mining.
    - Industrial demand soared. Foundries, steamships, and railways all needed coal. Mining villages sprang up, sometimes owned by colliery proprietors who paid workers in "truck" systems (partial wages in company goods).
    - Miner conditions were punishing: long hours, risk of cave-ins or gas explosions, minimal safety regulations. Despite these hazards, the lure of steady wages drew rural folk into pit communities.
2. **Iron Founding and Casting**
    - Access to local coal and ironstone led to ironworks expansions from the late 18th century onwards. Carron Iron

Works near Falkirk, founded in 1759, became renowned for cannons (the "carronade"), stoves, pots, and other cast-iron goods.
    - The hot-blast furnace invention by James Beaumont Neilson (1828) in Glasgow area drastically reduced fuel consumption, lowering production costs. Iron output skyrocketed, spurring locomotive and machinery manufacturing.
3. **Steel and Heavy Engineering**
    - By the mid-19th century, steelmaking advanced, though initially overshadowed by English centers like Sheffield. In Scotland, continuing improvements in metallurgy fostered machine-tool firms and locomotive works.
    - Glasgow's engineering firms, e.g., Neilson & Co., evolved into major suppliers of equipment for railways worldwide. This synergy between iron, steel, and mechanical engineering helped Glasgow earn the moniker "Workshop of the Empire."
4. **Urban and Regional Impact**
    - The concentration of coal mines, iron foundries, and engineering plants in the central belt (Lanarkshire, Glasgow outskirts) made this zone the industrial heart of Scotland. A belt of sooty towns and smoky chimneys formed along the Clyde, reminiscent of the "Black Country" in England.
    - Transport improvements—canals (like the Forth and Clyde Canal, completed 1790), and later railways—integrated resources, factories, and ports, stimulating further industrial sprawl. By the early 19th century, Glasgow overtook Edinburgh as Scotland's largest city, driven by heavy industry and trade.

Thus, a robust synergy of mining, metallurgy, and machine-building anchored Scotland's rise as an industrial engine, forging an industrial identity that contrasted with the earlier Enlightenment's philosophical glow.

5. Shipbuilding and Maritime Expansion

Because of its maritime tradition, Scotland also became a global force in shipbuilding:

1. **Clyde Shipyards**
    - The River Clyde, already central to tobacco importing, evolved into a major shipbuilding hub. Early yards built wooden vessels for coastal trade; after about 1812, iron-hulled ships began emerging. By the 1840s–1850s, Clyde shipyards embraced steam-powered, iron-clad craft, making them worldwide leaders.
    - Firms like Robert Napier & Sons specialized in marine engines, while others built clippers and steamers for transatlantic lines. Skilled labor in riveters, platers, and marine engineers converged along the Clyde's banks.
2. **Fishery and Coastal Towns**
    - The maritime economy extended well beyond the Clyde. On the east coast, ports such as Aberdeen, Peterhead, and Montrose thrived on fishing (herring especially). Over time, some fishing harbors also developed small-scale shipyards.
    - The expansion of shipping created job opportunities in seafaring and dock labor, though cyclical economic downturns and competition with English ports sometimes undermined growth.
3. **Links to Empire**
    - Scottish-built ships served the expanding British Empire, carrying goods, settlers, and raw materials between continents. Glasgow's shipping lines made it a gateway for emigration to North America and Australasia. The synergy of engineering, finance, and global trade endowed Scotland with an outsized role in forging Britain's imperial network.

Shipbuilding thus illustrated Scotland's transition to a full industrial powerhouse, bridging heavy manufacturing, maritime commerce, and engineering prowess.

6. Urban Growth, Housing, and Social Conditions

With industrial expansion came rapid urbanization, especially in the central belt:

1. **Population Explosion**
    - Scotland's population soared from around 1.3 million in 1750 to over 2 million by 1800, and continued climbing into the mid-19th century. Much of this growth concentrated in industrial districts like Glasgow, Paisley, Lanarkshire coalfields, and parts of the Lothians.
    - Rural-to-urban migration was spurred by the enclosure of farmland, the decline of small tenancies, and the lure of factory or mining wages.
2. **Tenement Living**
    - Many working-class families crammed into overcrowded tenement blocks. In Glasgow's poorer quarters, it was not uncommon to find multiple families sharing a single building "close," with inadequate sanitation.
    - Disease outbreaks (cholera, typhus) recurred, highlighting the public health crisis in congested urban zones. Middle-class reformers began calling for improved water supply, sewers, and slum clearance by the 1830s–1840s.
3. **Neighborhood Segregation**
    - Industrial cities became socially stratified. Wealthy entrepreneurs built grand houses in more pleasant suburbs or west-end districts. Skilled artisans lived in modestly better neighborhoods, while unskilled laborers crowded into the oldest, dankest city center lanes.
    - This spatial pattern created distinct class-based enclaves, intensifying social tensions.
4. **Moral and Religious Oversight**
    - Churches of various denominations (the established Kirk, Seceder groups, Methodists) launched missionary efforts in slums, offering Sunday schools, charities, and moral guidance. They viewed industrial working classes as at spiritual and moral risk.
    - Philanthropic societies also emerged, distributing food, clothing, and medical relief. Employers sometimes

contributed to these charities, seeing them as a bulwark against unrest.

Urban conditions thus presented both challenges and opportunities: a vibrant labor force for factories, but also squalor, disease, and social conflict. The contradictions of industrial progress—wealth for some, misery for many—became starkly visible in Scottish cities.

---

7. The Emergence of a Scottish Working Class

Industrialization reshaped class structures, creating a growing proletariat:

1. **Wage Labor in Mills and Mines**
    - Traditional forms of labor (like tenant farming or craft guild membership) waned as thousands joined factories or pit work for wages. The discipline of the factory bell replaced seasonal rhythms.
    - Women and children constituted a large share of the early textile workforce, with men more prevalent in heavy industries (iron, shipyards, mines). This gendered labor distribution influenced household economics, with women's earnings often crucial to family survival.
2. **Artisan Protests and Trade Societies**
    - Skilled trades, such as engineers, carpenters, printers, formed early "friendly societies" or "trade clubs" to help members in sickness or unemployment. Over time, these bodies evolved into trade unions.
    - Handloom weavers, threatened by mechanized looms, led some of the earliest labor agitations. In the 1820s–1830s, they staged strikes and sometimes destructive protests against mills. Government crackdowns on "combination" (unionizing) were harsh.
3. **Chartism and Radical Politics**
    - Inspired by calls for political reform in Britain, many Scottish workers supported the Chartist movement (1838–1848), which demanded universal male suffrage, secret ballots, and annual Parliaments.

- Scottish towns had strong Chartist associations, organizing mass rallies and petition campaigns. Although these demands were not fully met at the time, Chartism's influence left a lasting imprint on working-class consciousness.

4. **Social Life and Culture**
    - Despite poverty, workers forged strong communal bonds. Tenement stoops, shared washhouses, and local taverns were social gathering points. Self-help reading rooms and improvement societies popped up, reflecting a thirst for education.
    - Religious revivals also permeated the working class, with revivalist preachers galvanizing emotional responses to the hardships of industrial life.

Thus, an embryonic labor movement and a distinct working-class culture emerged, sowing seeds for future political and social reforms.

---

8. Regional Discrepancies: The Highlands vs. The Industrial Belt

While the Lowlands industrialized, the Highlands faced different trajectories:

1. **Limited Industrial Penetration**
    - Geographic isolation and sparse transportation networks (few roads or canals) meant heavy industry found little foothold north of the Highland line. Fishing, kelp gathering, and subsistence farming remained mainstays.
    - Some attempts at manufacturing—like cotton spinning in Inverness or woolens in northern towns—remained small-scale, overshadowed by the central belt's concentration of capital.
2. **Clanship Erosion and the Clearances**
    - The clan system was already weakened post-1745, and many chieftains, adopting "improvement" mentalities, sought to convert communal farmland into sheep pastures. The "Highland Clearances" began in the late 18th century, accelerating in the early 19th.

- Thousands of tenant families were forcibly evicted, prompting migrations either to Lowland cities or overseas. These rural upheavals contrasted with the industrial boom, forging a sense of Highland dispossession.
3. **Hebridean Realities**
    - Island communities in the Hebrides depended on seasonal fishing, crofting, and kelp burning. Fluctuating prices for kelp (used in soap and glass manufacture) left local populations vulnerable to collapse of markets.
    - Some landlords sought to replicate Lowland "improvements," ignoring Gaelic traditions. This tension fueled further emigration, particularly to Canada.

This divergence between the prosperous industrial Lowlands and the dispossessed Highlands formed a stark duality in 19th-century Scotland, shaping national debates about land rights, cultural identity, and economic justice.

---

9. Intellectual Reflections on Industry and Society

While the Scottish Enlightenment's heyday receded by the early 19th century, intellectuals continued analyzing industrialization:

1. **Political Economists and Philosophers**
    - After Adam Smith's era, new scholars built upon or critiqued the "Wealth of Nations." Some pointed to negative social externalities (child labor, slum conditions) as requiring moral or state intervention.
    - Thinkers like Thomas Chalmers (a minister and economist) argued for philanthropic and church-based solutions to urban poverty, reflecting a moral philanthropic approach to industrial society's ills.
2. **Romantic Reactions**
    - Writers like Sir Walter Scott (1771–1832), though historically focused on medieval or Jacobite themes, indirectly offered romantic nostalgia for a pre-industrial Scotland. This fed middle-class fascination with Highland folklore and "traditional" life.

- Meanwhile, poetry and literature sometimes praised the triumph of progress, though some verses lamented the loss of rural community. A tension arose between a celebratory modernism and a longing for older, more "authentic" Scotland.
3. **Early Sociological Observations**
    - Observers from continental Europe visited the Glasgow region, noting vast differences in wealth, squalor, and social discipline. Scottish pamphleteers and journalists wrote tracts describing the plight of miners or child factory workers, stirring calls for legislative remedies.

While no single intellectual movement rivaled the earlier Enlightenment's cohesive impact, a broad discourse developed, grappling with the blessings and curses of rapid industrial change.

---

10. Conclusion

From the late 18th through the early 19th centuries, Scotland's embrace of mechanized industry dramatically reconfigured its economy, social fabric, and landscapes. Textile mills, iron foundries, shipyards, and coal pits made the central belt a crucible of progress—and exploitation. Booming cities like Glasgow drew in rural migrants, forging a vibrant working-class culture but also squalid slums and labor unrest. Meanwhile, the Highlands and islands, largely bypassed by heavy industry, experienced their own crises through the Clearances, as tenants were uprooted to make way for commercial sheep farms.

This Industrial Revolution integrated Scotland more fully into the burgeoning British economy, generating wealth for merchants, investors, and industrialists while sowing dislocation and hardship for many laborers. Over time, these tensions sparked reform campaigns, trade unionism, and philanthropic initiatives aimed at mitigating the worst conditions. The next chapter (**Chapter 20**) will look at how these forces unfolded in the 19th century, shaping political reforms, driving emigration to far-flung corners of the empire, and continuing to transform Scotland's national identity. Through it all, the interplay between tradition and innovation would define this crucial epoch, leaving a complex legacy of resilience, enterprise, and social challenges for modern Scotland.

CHAPTER 20

REFORM, EMIGRATION, AND A CHANGING SCOTLAND

1. Introduction

By the early 19th century, Scotland had emerged as a significant player in Britain's industrial and imperial systems, with bustling urban centers in the Lowlands and deep social cleavages between wealthy industrialists and impoverished workers. Simultaneously, the rural Highlands faced upheaval through the Clearances, compelling many Gaelic-speaking Scots to migrate. Against this backdrop, the nation confronted pressures for political reform, spurred in part by the working-class movements and liberal ideals taking root across Britain. From parliamentary acts granting broader representation to the large-scale emigration of Scots to North America and beyond, the country underwent profound shifts in identity and social structure.

In this final chapter of our historical arc, we will examine the drive for political changes—like the Reform Acts of the 19th century—and the factors that propelled thousands of Scots to seek new lives overseas. We will consider how these emigrants influenced global diaspora networks and how their departures impacted local communities. Finally, we will look at the transformations that set the stage for Scotland's modern era: from the growth of civic institutions to the evolving relationships between Highland tradition and urban industrial society. Through reform and emigration, Scotland carved new paths for its people, reshaping national identity in the process.

---

2. The Push for Political Reform

Well into the 19th century, Scotland's political representation remained limited, with property restrictions on voting and the continued dominance of landowning elites in parliamentary seats:

1. **The Pre-Reform Landscape**

- After the Acts of Union (1707), Scotland sent only 45 MPs to the House of Commons. Voting qualifications were narrow; most adult men had no franchise. In burgh constituencies, small groups of local councilors or guild members chose MPs, while in county constituencies, only a handful of major landowners had votes.
- This system, rife with patronage and nepotism, was increasingly challenged by a rising middle class of merchants, industrialists, and professionals who demanded a say in governance.

2. **Radical and Reform Movements**
    - The 1790s saw radical "Friends of the People" societies, inspired by the French Revolution, call for universal male suffrage. Government crackdowns stifled such agitation.
    - Post-Napoleonic War depression in 1815–1820 revived demands for reform, culminating in events like the "Radical War" of 1820, where small groups of weavers and artisans attempted insurrection in central Scotland. The government swiftly suppressed them, executing or transporting leaders.

3. **The Reform Act of 1832**
    - Growing public support and fear of mass unrest persuaded the British Parliament to pass the Reform Act of 1832. This measure expanded the electorate, redistributing seats to reflect newer industrial towns. In Scotland, the electorate rose from about 4,500 men to some 65,000.
    - Although still far from universal suffrage, the Reform Act gave a voice to some middle-class citizens in thriving industrial burghs like Glasgow, Paisley, and Dundee, diminishing aristocratic control. It also signaled the principle that parliamentary representation should evolve with societal changes.

4. **Further Reforms**
    - Subsequent acts in 1867, 1884, and beyond incrementally broadened the franchise, allowing more working-class men to vote. Scotland's urban populations gained greater political weight.
    - While many conservatives feared mob rule or Jacobin radicalism, the moderate liberal tradition that emerged in

Scotland typically balanced calls for progressive reform with respect for property rights and monarchy.

Thus, political reform advanced slowly but steadily, reflecting the interplay of rising industrial classes, persistent radical movements, and cautious parliamentary maneuvering in London.

---

3. Chartism and the Working Class

In the middle decades of the 19th century, Scotland's working class participated vigorously in the British Chartist movement:

1. **Scottish Chartist Organizations**
    - Weavers, miners, ironworkers, and other laborers embraced the People's Charter (1838) demanding universal male suffrage, secret ballots, annual parliaments, and other democratic reforms.
    - Cities like Glasgow and Dundee hosted mass Chartist rallies, with tens of thousands attending. Petitions bearing thousands of Scottish signatures joined national submissions to Parliament.
2. **Internal Divisions**
    - Chartism encompassed moderate "moral force" advocates, who sought peaceful lobbying and petitioning, and "physical force" radicals more open to confrontation.
    - Some of Scotland's laboring men, embittered by continued low wages and factory discipline, leaned toward more militant stances, yet large-scale violence was rare. Government watchers monitored these groups closely.
3. **Outcome of Chartism**
    - Parliament rejected the giant Chartist petitions in 1839, 1842, and 1848. Despite these failures, Chartism left behind a legacy of mass political consciousness, establishing trade union networks and stirring debates on social justice.
    - Gradual reforms in the later 19th century (like the 1867 and 1884 Reform Acts) eventually implemented many demands

on suffrage, though not in the radical form envisioned by early Chartists.

Through Chartism, Scottish laborers honed organizational skills, fueling an enduring tradition of labor activism and forging alliances with liberal reformers who recognized that industrial society demanded fair representation.

---

4. The Highland Clearances and Rural Transformation

While Lowland industrialization and urban reform captured much attention, the rural Highlands underwent wrenching upheaval:

1. **Origins of the Clearances**
    - Post-1745, many clan chiefs embraced "improvement" doctrines. Traditional communal farming (runrig, shared grazing) seemed antiquated to lairds seeking higher rents. Sheep farming, driven by demand for wool in southern markets, offered greater profits.
    - Beginning in the late 18th century, entire glens were cleared of small tenants (crofters), who were relocated to coastal villages for fishing or forced to emigrate. The largest wave occurred between ~1780 and ~1850.
2. **Social and Cultural Impact**
    - Displaced families lost not only land but also centuries-old Gaelic community structures. Gaelic language and traditions eroded as people scattered to new areas.
    - Some Clearances were brutal, with homes burned, herds scattered, or forced marches to the coast. While not universally violent, the process typically lacked meaningful compensation. Many Gaelic songs and stories lament these tragic evictions.
3. **Emigration to the Colonies**
    - Large numbers of Highlanders sought better opportunities abroad—Canada (Nova Scotia, Cape Breton), the United States, Australia. Shiploads of emigrants left in "coffin

ships," often subsidized by lairds who preferred removing tenants over maintaining them on impoverished plots.
    - This diaspora spread Gaelic culture overseas, forming tight-knit communities in Cape Breton or Ontario that preserved certain customs. However, the severing from ancestral lands caused deep cultural trauma.
4. **Lowland Agriculture**
    - In parallel, Lowland estates continued enclosure and mechanization. Many small tenant farmers migrated to towns, while wealthier tenant farmers expanded into bigger holdings. The rural Lowlands thus stabilized around modern farming, while the Highlands reeled from the Clearances' social disruption.

Hence, the Clearances represent a stark transformation of Highland society—an event reverberating through Scottish memory, shaping diaspora narratives, and highlighting the divide between progressive landowner economics and communal Gaelic traditions.

---

5. The Great Emigration Waves (19th Century)

Beyond the Highlands, many Scots of varying backgrounds chose to leave the country:

1. **Industrial Migrants**
    - Economic booms and busts in Scottish mills and mines prompted some workers to seek steadier employment overseas. Skilled artisans or engineers found openings in the United States, where the building of canals, railways, and factories needed expertise.
    - By the mid-19th century, improved steamship travel eased transatlantic journeys, spurring more frequent relocations.
2. **Urban Overcrowding and Poverty**
    - The hardships of city life—unemployment, slum conditions, disease—compelled certain families to gamble on a new life in North America or Australia. Emigration societies and

philanthropic groups occasionally offered subsidized passages for the destitute.
3. **Colonial Opportunities**
    - The British Empire's expansion into Canada, India, South Africa, and Australasia created demand for administrators, soldiers, merchants, and farmers. Scots capitalized on these roles, building influential enclaves abroad.
    - Examples include the Canadian fur trade (dominated by Scots in the North West Company) and the engineering projects in India's railways. Emigrant Scots often maintained strong cultural ties—e.g., founding Caledonian societies or Gaelic churches.
4. **Personal and Cultural Motives**
    - Some left seeking religious freedom if they belonged to minority sects (e.g., certain Presbyterians or Episcopalians). Others yearned for adventure or land ownership unattainable in a stratified homeland.
    - Letters from successful emigrants, describing relative prosperity, spurred chain migrations, pulling more kin and neighbors across the seas.

By the mid- to late 19th century, Scotland's diaspora extended across the globe, forging both emotional ties to the old country and material networks funneling remittances home. Emigration thus relieved some domestic population pressures but also sparked concerns about "brain drain" or the loss of Gaelic communities.

---

6. Religious Diversity and Free Church Movements

Meanwhile, within Scotland, new religious currents shaped social life:

1. **Disruption of 1843**
    - A major ecclesiastical rift known as the "Disruption" occurred when roughly a third of the Church of Scotland's ministers, led by Dr. Thomas Chalmers, broke away to form the Free Church of Scotland. They objected to the state's

interference in parish appointments (the patronage system) and insisted that congregations choose their own ministers.
- This schism reverberated across communities. Many lairds who backed the established church ejected Free Church worshippers from local buildings, forcing them to erect "Free Kirk" chapels, sometimes in makeshift settings. The Disruption mirrored deeper tensions between liberal demands for popular governance and conservative institutions.

2. **Continuing Sectarian Divides**
    - Episcopalian pockets (sometimes associated with Jacobitism in older days) survived, especially in parts of the northeast. Catholic populations, historically small outside the western Highlands, grew in the 19th century due to Irish immigration—workers arriving to build canals, railways, and in flight from the Irish Famine (1840s).
    - This influx of Irish Catholic laborers spurred occasional sectarian friction, particularly in industrial towns like Glasgow, foreshadowing the later "Old Firm" divisions in Scottish sporting culture. Church expansions among the Catholic community revitalized a tradition repressed since the Reformation.

3. **Religion and Social Reform**
    - Churches played vital roles in education, philanthropy, and moral campaigning. Sunday schools, temperance societies, and mission halls aimed to uplift the poor, reflecting the era's evangelical zeal.
    - The "Free Church" and other dissenting denominations, though initially formed around ecclesiastical issues, often championed political reforms, forging alliances with liberal MPs who favored expanded suffrage and social legislation.

Thus, religious diversity intensified, shaped by doctrinal splits, Irish immigration, and continuing Presbyterian energies. The 19th-century "evangelical wave" coexisted with industrial modernity, influencing everything from schooling to charity.

7. Changing Gender Roles and Family Life

Scotland's industrial and emigrant contexts also touched upon women's roles:

1. **Millwork and Domestic Service**
    - Women formed a large share of the workforce in textile factories, paid lower wages than men. They often balanced jobs with family responsibilities, placing strain on domestic life.
    - Many young women from rural areas found employment as domestic servants in middle- or upper-class households in Edinburgh or Glasgow, living in "service." This offered a measure of financial independence but also subjection to paternalistic control.
2. **Moral and Social Campaigning**
    - Certain women participated in philanthropic or religious societies, raising funds for missions, poor relief, or temperance. These activities granted them a public voice, albeit channeled through "feminine" charitable spheres.
    - A handful of women's advocates, influenced by broader British debates, began questioning legal restrictions on women's property rights or educational opportunities. By the mid-19th century, small stirrings of a Scottish women's movement emerged, though overshadowed by mainstream liberal politics.
3. **Emigration and Family**
    - In Highland clearances or overseas flights, women played pivotal roles managing clan networks or supporting family farms. Once in Canada or Australia, they helped build new "Scottish" communities, preserving Gaelic language or Presbyterian worship.
    - The separation of families, with husbands leaving first, sometimes created transatlantic family ties that shaped emotional and financial dependencies.

While no sweeping feminist upheavals occurred at this stage, the seeds of changing gender relations were sown, becoming more visible toward the latter half of the century.

8. Movement Toward Broader Education and Literacy

Inspired by industrial progress and religious zeal, Scotland made strides in education:

1. **Parish Schools and Kirk Influence**
   - Since the Reformation, parish schools had taught basic literacy to children (especially boys), fueling Scotland's reputation for relatively high literacy rates. In the 19th century, philanthropic and church bodies expanded these schools, though quality varied widely.
   - In industrial towns, Sunday schools and ragged schools attempted to educate street children, many of whom worked throughout the week.
2. **Mechanics' Institutes**
   - Mechanics' institutes emerged in places like Glasgow and Edinburgh, offering evening lectures on science, technology, and literature for working men. These institutes aimed to produce a disciplined, skilled labor force capable of handling new industrial technology.
   - Some members of the middle class saw such programs as a means to moralize and pacify the laboring classes, though many workers genuinely appreciated the chance to learn.
3. **Universities and Reform**
   - The ancient universities began modernizing admissions and curricula further in the early 19th century, though still catering mostly to middle- and upper-class males. Calls for broader access resulted in incremental changes, setting the stage for expansions in the later 19th century.

This educational ferment contributed to Scotland's continuing reputation for an educated populace, bridging Enlightenment ideals with industrial society's practical demands.

9. Political Shifts Post-1850: Liberal Hegemony

By mid-century, liberal politics became dominant in much of Lowland Scotland:

1. **Expanding the Franchise**
   - The Reform Acts of 1867 and 1884 further enlarged the electorate, granting many urban workers the vote. Scottish constituencies returned liberal MPs who championed free trade, religious nonconformity, and gradual social reform.
   - Notable liberal figures, such as William Ewart Gladstone (an English MP, but popular in Scotland), found strong support in Scottish towns that prized progress and moral improvement.
2. **Decline of Toryism in Urban Centers**
   - The Conservative (Tory) Party struggled to appeal to expanding industrial populations, though it retained pockets of support among aristocrats, landed gentry, and some rural parishes.
   - The old "laird-led" politics that had dominated pre-reform Scotland gave way to more modern party structures and populist election campaigns.
3. **Rise of Local Governance**
   - Municipal corporations in cities like Glasgow took on new roles: water supply, public sanitation, policing. Glasgow's city fathers, proud of civic improvement, built grand municipal buildings, advanced waterworks (Loch Katrine project), and championed public health measures.
   - This municipal activism paralleled the push for "civic gospel" in other British cities, underscoring how an industrial society demanded new forms of governance.

Hence, 19th-century reform aligned Scotland's institutions more closely with those of liberal Britain, reinforcing the union's ties while still preserving a distinct sense of regional politics and identity.

10. Conclusion

Across the 19th century, Scotland underwent far-reaching changes in governance, social structure, and population distribution. The impetus for parliamentary reform—driven by radical working-class movements, middle-class liberals, and cautious elites—gradually extended political representation, culminating in a predominantly liberal political culture by mid- to late century. Meanwhile, the ongoing Highland Clearances and broader emigration waves reshaped not only local Highland societies but also planted Scottish communities across the globe, forging diaspora connections that endure to this day. Religious schisms like the Disruption of 1843 demonstrated the continued potency of faith in shaping national debates, even as industrial modernity advanced.

By the 1850s and beyond, Scotland's place in the world had shifted from a primarily agrarian kingdom to an integral part of the world's foremost industrial and imperial power. Cities swelled with factory workers, and philanthropic or radical voices pressed for improvements in labor conditions, housing, and education. Gaelic-speaking Highland communities diminished numerically, their traditions scattered by clearance or assimilation. In sum, the era of reform and emigration irrevocably transformed Scotland, preparing the ground for the late 19th and early 20th centuries, when further challenges—from empire, global competition, and political movements—would continue to shape the nation's destiny.

Printed in Great Britain
by Amazon